Mendelssohn
His Life and Music

www.naxos.com/naxosbooks/mendelssohnlifeandmusic

by Neil Wenborn

Mendelssohn
His Life and Music

For my parents
Audrey and Arthur
with love and gratitude

Author's Acknowledgements

The Mendelssohns were one of the most documented families of their time, both by their own and by others' pens. This book draws on several sources for translations of Mendelssohn's and his friends' and family's correspondence, as well as of contemporary accounts and other primary material. The author and publishers gratefully acknowledge the originators of these translations, the sources of which are listed in the bibliography. My thanks are also due to Genevieve Helsby of Naxos Books for asking me to write the book and for seeing it into print, and to Anthony Short, who has once again proved the ideal editor – and, above all, to Sue and Edward as always for their patience and support.

Published by Naxos Books, an imprint of Naxos Rights International Ltd

© Naxos Books 2008

www.naxosbooks.com

Printed and bound in China by Leo Paper Group

Design and layout: Hannah Davies, Fruition – Creative Concepts

All photographs © Lebrecht Music & Arts Photo Library

Edited by Anthony Short

Front cover picture: Mendelssohn, by G. Jager

Front cover background picture: An illustration of Act IV, Scene 1 of Shakespeare's *A Midsummer Night's Dream*, with Tatiana, Bottom, Puck and fairies in the wood

Title page picture: Portrait of Mendelssohn by Eduard Magnus, 1845/6

A CIP Record for this book is available from the British Library.

ISBN: 978-1-84379-232-1

Contents

www.naxos.com/naxosbooks/mendelssohnlifeandmusic

Visit the dedicated website for *Mendelssohn: His Life and Music* and gain free access to the following:

Hours more music to listen to

Music by some of Mendelssohn's contemporaries

A timeline of Mendelssohn's life, set alongside contemporary events in arts, culture and politics

To access this you will need:

- ISBN: 9781843792321
- Password: Fingal

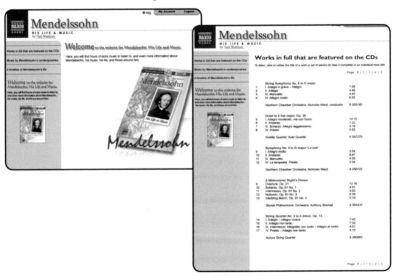

www.naxos.com/naxosbooks/mendelssohnlifeandmusic

Preface

Mendelssohn is an enigma. His best-known compositions – *The Hebrides*, the Violin Concerto, the 'Italian' Symphony – are among the most famous and most loved of all classical works. Some of his smaller pieces, indeed, have paid the price of over-familiarity. The 'Spring Song' from the piano *Songs without Words*, for example, or the soprano solo 'O for the wings of a dove' from the choral work *Hear My Prayer*, have been so popular for so long that it is now barely possible to recover their shine from under the tarnish of use. At the same time, Mendelssohn's reach extends far beyond the classical music lover. His music is the soundtrack to the happiest moments of millions of lives. Countless brides have walked up the aisle to the strains of his 'Wedding March'; while for generations of children and nostalgic adults *Hark! the herald angels sing* is as much a part of the ideal fabric of Christmas as mistletoe, sleigh bells and figgy pudding. These are among the world's most familiar melodies. But how many people could name Mendelssohn as their composer, let alone realise that their origins lie in the entr'acte music for a courtly production of a Shakespeare play and an obscure choral work celebrating the 400th anniversary of the invention of printing? More than a century and a half after his death, Mendelssohn's music is all around us. But he remains a hard composer to place.

He is hard to place in the history of music, too. Mendelssohn's life was tragically short, but it spanned a period of intense ferment both in his chosen art and in the wider world. When he was born, Haydn was living out his last months in a Vienna threatened by the forces of Napoleon. By the time of his death, just thirty-eight years later, Wagner was at work on *Lohengrin*, and the cataclysmic events that were to prove the birth-pangs of modern Europe – the revolutions of March 1848 – were only weeks away. Yet Mendelssohn himself stands curiously aloof from the dominant currents of his age, eluding categorisation. In the *New Grove* composer biography series he appears alongside Berlioz as one of the 'Early Romantic Masters'; but he was nothing if not a proud Classicist, devoted to the memory of Mozart and Haydn, and profoundly unsympathetic to what he saw as the attitudinising indiscipline of Berlioz's music. The product of a rigorous musical training with its roots in the teaching methods of Johann Sebastian Bach, he was the nineteenth century's pre-eminent interpreter of Bach and Handel, and his own music was second to none in channelling their legacy; but he was also a pioneering exponent of what would come to be known as 'programme music', the mistily evocative textures of his *Hebrides* overture providing a template for decades of Romantic tone-painting. Historicist, Classicist, Romantic: none of the labels fits, and yet they all do.

Felix Mendelssohn, then, was a composer of many faces. He was also astonishingly prolific. The catalogue of his works runs to some 400 items (more than a quarter of them written before his sixteenth birthday), not counting transcriptions and arrangements of other composers' works or the numerous canons he composed for relaxation or as gifts for friends. This trove of music includes examples of every major classical genre, though opera — ironically the form to which he aspired above all others — is represented only by works of his earliest youth. Yet Mendelssohn is almost unique among composers of his standing in that the majority of his output still remains virtually unknown. In this respect, the music of *Hark! the herald-angels sing* — a piece detached from its original context in a work now entirely forgotten — may stand as a microcosm of his entire oeuvre. The most familiar works are staples of the repertoire, as soundly embedded in the collective consciousness as any music ever written; the rest, to a remarkable extent, remain unheard. Sacred and secular choral works, solo songs, part-songs, incidental music, works for a variety of chamber combinations — all form a substantial part of his portfolio, but with a few exceptions they are rarely heard today in either the concert hall or the recording studio.

The trajectory of Mendelssohn's career is equally resistant to smooth patterning. He was once conventionally regarded as a composer who reached, in his seventeenth year, a summit of achievement from which the rest of his musical output was at best a declivity broken by occasional peaks. He has even been represented as a sort of Orson Welles of music, living his creative life in reverse, the Octet and the overture to *A Midsummer Night's Dream* his *Citizen Kane*, the ubiquitous *Songs without Words* his sherry advertisements. Modern scholarship has revealed him as a more consistent explorer of the musical landscape, forever testing the potential of the forms and social contexts in which he worked. But the radiance of those early masterpieces remains uniquely dazzling, and the shadows they cast are long enough to occlude works which would themselves be guarantors of immortality had they been written by anyone else. If his career represents a mismatch between promise and fulfilment, then, it is principally because the sheer lavishness of that promise was all but unprecedented. Surely the greatest child genius in the history of music, Mendelssohn has also been the prisoner of his own precocity.

No less labile is the course charted by Mendelssohn's posthumous reputation. By his mid-thirties he was almost routinely described as the world's greatest living composer, the natural heir to Mozart and Beethoven. His oratorios *St Paul* and *Elijah* were regarded as monuments of the creative spirit, while his *Songs without Words* stood open at the piano in drawing rooms throughout Europe and beyond. Within years of his death, however, the pendulum had begun to swing back the other way, helped in 1850 by a self-serving shove from Wagner's poisonous article *On Judaism in Music*. Thirty-odd years later an opinionated young music critic by the name of George Bernard Shaw administered another push in the same direction – though without the anti-Semitism – when he lambasted Mendelssohn's 'kid glove gentility, his conventional sentimentality, and his despicable oratorio mongering'. Above all, perhaps, Mendelssohn's reputation has suffered from the cultural equivalent of guilt by association. At home, the association was with a poet, Gottlieb Biedermeier, who published only after Mendelssohn's death and, to add insult to injury, didn't actually exist even then. Biedermeier, the fictional creation of two satirically minded students, gave a name to what they saw as the philistine conservatism of the German middle classes in the first half of the nineteenth century and thus also to the sensibilities of one of Mendelssohn's key domestic audiences. Similarly, abroad, Mendelssohn unwittingly yoked his reputation to the values of Victorian England. A sensation with London concertgoers, he was a regular guest at Buckingham Palace during his visits to Britain – 'that right little, tight little island', as he called it – and what Biedermeier was to his legacy in Germany, Shaw and Lytton Strachey would be to his reception in the English-speaking world. But the most sinister nemesis of all awaited him in Germany in the twentieth century. With Hitler's accession to power in 1933, Mendelssohn, as the product of a Jewish family, was written out of his nation's cultural history for the duration of Nazi rule.

This book traces the course of a remarkable life. It used to be axiomatic that Mendelssohn's privileged background somehow exempted him not just from material need but also from a species of practical and emotional struggle essential to the creation of truly great music. 'Since contented nations and contented men have no history,' wrote the critic Émile Vuillermoz, 'one should on principle abandon the idea of writing a life of Mendelssohn.' Mendelssohn's was, according to this school of thought, a life without significant incident. Everything came easily to him, including music. Certainly, as the grandson of the famous philosopher Moses Mendelssohn and the son of the wealthy and staggeringly well-connected banker Abraham Mendelssohn, Felix was born to prominence and security. But his life could hardly have been a less leisured one.

Brought up from the earliest age to fill every minute of the day with intellectually gainful activity, he carried into adulthood an almost pathological incapacity for idleness. His professional life was far from confined to composition. Indeed, creative work was increasingly relegated to the margins of his manifold other responsibilities, which included those of conductor, administrator, teacher and editor. He made lasting contributions to the practice of music in every area of his professional activity. As editor of the works of Bach and Handel, he introduced – generations ahead of his time – the concept of strict faithfulness to the authorial manuscript. As an administrator of extraordinary drive and vision, he concerned himself with the social welfare of his musicians, campaigning for better working conditions and pension rights. And as a conductor, he moved the art of directing an orchestra beyond time-beating to interpretation, while his programming practice made him perhaps the single most significant force in the development of the concept of a European musical canon. He was, into the bargain, an inveterate walker, mountaineer and swimmer, a prolific and accomplished artist, and the writer of thousands of letters, many of which could easily be repackaged as travel literature. As if all that were not enough to absorb his energies, he was also the fully involved father of a family of five children, and a man whose social life reflected the high visibility of his public profile.

Nor did music itself come as easily to him as some detractors have believed. His self-confessed 'awful reverence for print' led to a habit of compulsive revision, bedevilling both the chronology of his compositions, which were often revisited over several years, and the numbering of his published works. (Every Opus up to and including 72 was published during his lifetime; everything from 73 upwards – including such major works as the 'Italian' and 'Reformation' Symphonies – was issued after his death.) That he was unable to concentrate exclusively on composition was a source of increasing torment to him in his final years. Not the least remarkable thing about Mendelssohn, however, given what else he managed to cram into his short life, is that he found the time and energy to write any music at all. Far from being oases of comfort and ease, then, his days were crowded with activity to – and ultimately beyond –

the limits of his very considerable strength. His death mask shows, shockingly, the face of a man aged far beyond his thirty-eight years.

Finally, a strange coda. In November 1936, on a concert tour of Germany, Sir Thomas Beecham visited the monument to Mendelssohn that had stood for more than forty years in front of the institution most closely associated with him, the Leipzig Gewandhaus. The following day Beecham returned with a group of musicians to a lay a wreath to the great man. The statue was gone, torn down in the night on the orders of a local Nazi functionary. It is an unsettling story, resonant with the terrible capriciousness of twentieth-century cultural politics and the provisional nature of all repute, but also, somehow, with the fundamental elusiveness of Mendelssohn as a composer. It has a sequel, though. On 10 March 1993 the Leipzig authorities unveiled a new statue of Mendelssohn, this time outside the Neues Gewandhaus. There is still, in a sense, a gap where Mendelssohn should be. But perhaps in the end his enigma is the enigma of all great art: its capacity to offer a new face, and different perspectives, to each new generation of devotees.

Mendelssohn: His Life and Music

Chapter 1

The Wunderkind
(1809–1825)

The Wunderkind (1809–1825)

'We have a certain amount of joy in this young man,' Abraham Mendelssohn wrote to his wife Lea, with characteristic sobriety, in 1833, 'and I often think: long live Martens' Mill!'

The young man in question was Abraham's eldest son Felix, then twenty-four years old and already celebrated as a composer set fair to rank with Bach, Mozart and Beethoven in the future annals of German music. Martens' Mill, by contrast, belonged to the family's past. A balconied cottage on the river Elbe, it was where Abraham and Lea had spent the summers of their early married life, dividing their time between it and nearby Hamburg, where Abraham was building a career (and a fortune) for himself in the family banking business. Hamburg was the city of the composer's birth; but on the evidence of his father's letter it was at Martens' Mill the previous summer that the course of Mendelssohn's short and extraordinarily active life began.

A composer's place of conception may seem excessively privileged information. In the case of Mendelssohn, however, it scarcely answers the biographer's perennial question of where to start. It is a truism that an artist's life, like anyone else's, is shaped by his or her background. But for Mendelssohn that background exerted a more than usually inescapable influence, not only on his personality and the shape of his creative career, but also on the reception of his music both

The 'German Socrates': Mendelssohn's grandfather Moses Mendelssohn, c. 1780

during his lifetime and since. He was the scion of one of the most extraordinary families of his time – memorably described by one American critic, the late Herbert Kupferberg, as 'the Rothschilds of culture' – and the history and traditions of that family profoundly informed his sense of himself and of his place in the world.

Had Felix never written a note of music, the name of Mendelssohn would still be famous today. The composer's grandfather, Moses Mendelssohn, was a central presence in the European Enlightenment and a pivotal figure in the troubled history of Jewish–Christian relations. Even stripped of its accretions of myth, his story remains the stuff of fiction, and implausible fiction at that. Born in the poverty and oppression of the Dessau ghetto in 1729, Moses, who replaced his given name, Moses ben Mendel Dessau, with the name Mendelssohn, rose to become one of the foremost thinkers of his generation. Aesthetician, philosopher, biblical translator and unofficial ambassador for European Jewry, he was also a respected businessman, succeeding his employer in the management of a thriving silk factory. He was an intimate friend of the dramatist Gotthold Ephraim Lessing (who modelled on him the eponymous hero of his play *Nathan the Wise*), a scholar whose translation of the Pentateuch into German was a seminal force in the Jewish Enlightenment or *Haskalah*, and a voice for tolerance whose humanity resonates as movingly at the beginning of the twenty-first century as it did at the end of the eighteenth. His philosophical treatise *Phaedon*, which was translated into every major European language, became the unlikely bestseller of its age, and earned him, a Jew by birth and lifelong practice, the epithet of 'the German Socrates'. Kant hailed him as a genius who would usher in 'a new epoch in philosophy', and by the time of his death in 1786 he was known as 'the third Moses' in direct succession to the lawgiver and the twelfth-century philosopher Moses Maimonides, whose *Guide for the Perplexed* had been a decisive influence on his thinking as a youth in Dessau. All this he achieved by sheer force of intellect and personality, and against a background of physical disability and of strictures on Jews that remained substantially unchanged since medieval times.

Not until 1763, when he was thirty-four years old, did Moses Mendelssohn receive 'privileged' status (which conferred some basic rights, such as the right to own property) in his adoptive Prussia. The year after the philosopher's death, however, the new king Frederick William II extended the same status to his widow and descendants. Moses' six surviving children thus inherited a position in European cultural and social life that would have been unimaginable to their father when he set out on foot for

Berlin forty-five years earlier. It was a legacy they deployed with sometimes explosive independence of mind.

Moses' eldest child, his daughter Brendel, was a key player in the salon life of late-eighteenth-century Berlin. Educated by her father, who arranged her marriage to a respectable banker, she was a woman of enormous intellectual accomplishment and a close friend of the legendary salon hostesses Henriette Herz and Rahel Levin Varnhagen. She also became one of the most scandalous figures of her time: in 1798 she left her husband and sons to set up home with the erratic writer and critic Friedrich Schlegel, one of the pioneers of German Romanticism, whom she eventually married. In a move that would have further scandalised her father, Brendel also converted, first to Protestantism and then to Catholicism, adopting the name Dorothea. Ostracised by many of her relatives and former friends, she was nonetheless the only Mendelssohn to be present at the wedding of her nephew Felix in 1837.

The life of Dorothea's sister Henriette – Felix's Aunt Jette – would also be remembered for scandal, though not in this case of her own making. As highly connected as her sister, and like her a convert to Catholicism, Henriette counted among her friends such luminaries of the age as Madame de Staël, Benjamin Constant and the composer Gaspare Spontini. Much of her career was spent in Paris, where she lived in some splendour as the governess to Fanny Sebastiani, the headstrong daughter of one of Napoleon's generals. It was Fanny's unhappy fate to become the victim of one of the nineteenth century's most notorious crimes of passion: in 1847, sixteen years after Henriette had died, Fanny was stabbed to death by her unfaithful husband, the Duke of Choiseul-Praslin, who committed suicide in his prison cell before he could stand trial.

The 'human hyphen': the composer's father Abraham Mendelssohn

The eldest sons of Moses Mendelssohn, Joseph and Abraham, led less colourful but equally distinguished lives. Both pursued careers in banking, Joseph in Berlin and Abraham in Paris, before entering into partnership together in Berlin in 1804 and in Hamburg the following year: the Mendelssohn Brothers bank became one of Germany's leading financial institutions, remaining in business until its forced closure by the Nazis in 1938. Also in 1804 Abraham married Lea Salomon, the eminence of whose family eclipsed even that of the Mendelssohns. Lea was the granddaughter of Daniel Itzig, who had made his fortune as court banker to Frederick the Great. The first Jew ever to be granted Prussian citizenship, Itzig oversaw the financing of the monarch's intervention in the Seven Years War, and his fabulous wealth was matched by a degree of access to circles of power and influence virtually unprecedented for a practising Jew of his time and place. Lea grew up on one of Itzig's Berlin properties, the Bartholdy dairy farm which would later provide Felix with his baptismal surname, and seems to have matched her high-achieving relatives in cultural accomplishments, including the command of several languages and an aptitude for music. She was a gifted conversationalist, had a good singing voice and could give a creditable account of the keyboard works of J.S. Bach, whose sons Wilhelm Friedemann and Carl Philipp Emanuel had been respectively the teacher and protégé of her formidable aunt, the long-lived Berlin *salonnière* Sarah Levy.

This, then, was the remarkable clan into which Felix Mendelssohn was born on 3 February 1809, the second of Abraham and Lea's four children. His elder sister Fanny had been born in 1805; another sister, Rebecka, was born in 1811 and a brother, Paul, the following year.

For all the preternatural powers of recall he was soon to demonstrate, Felix is unlikely to have remembered the most dramatic episode of his early childhood. As a thriving free port, Hamburg was a significant entrepôt for British goods. When, in 1806, Napoleon imposed the so-called Continental System – the blockade of European ports by which he hoped to strangle British trade with the Continent – the Mendelssohn brothers, like many others, seem to have been active in undermining it by extending their business activities to include some profitable smuggling. It was probably for this reason that, soon after Napoleon's forces occupied Hamburg at the beginning of 1811 in an attempt to enforce the blockade, Abraham and Lea fled the city incognito with their children, including the two-year-old Felix. By the beginning of July the Mendelssohns were back in Berlin, which was to provide the family with its centre of gravity for the rest of Abraham's and Lea's lives and beyond.

The Prussian capital in 1811 was not an obvious choice of refuge from French authority. Like Hamburg, the city was under French occupation, and Prussia, truncated by Napoleon's territorial depredations, had effectively been a puppet state of the Republic since King Frederick William III's defeat at the Battle of Jena five years earlier. The reforming spirit of Napoleonic rule could bring certain social advantages, not least (as Abraham had discovered as a young banker in Paris) for Jews, who were granted Prussian rights of citizenship under the Edict of Emancipation in 1812. By the same token, however, the anti-Napoleonic and increasingly self-consciously Christian thrust of resurgent German nationalism could all too easily express itself in anti-Semitism. The Mendelssohns were better insulated than most against attack from either camp – Aunt Sarah's contacts included the French ambassador to Prussia, and Abraham's sister Dorothea was a friend of the philosopher Johann Gottlieb Fichte, one of the founding fathers of German nationalism – but on at least one occasion the young Felix seems to have been jeered at in the street as a 'Jew-boy'.

A Francophile in Paris in the 1790s, Abraham proved himself a committed nationalist in the Berlin of the 1810s. As the tide turned against Napoleon with the Emperor's retreat from Russia in the winter of 1812, Prussia once again declared war on France, and the Mendelssohn bank helped to supply the Prussian army with guns and funded a military hospital to care for the wounded. All in all, the Mendelssohns did well out of the war. The bank gained in business and prestige – it was one of the financial institutions charged with overseeing the payment of French reparations after Napoleon's final defeat at Waterloo in 1815 – and Abraham himself was elected a city councillor.

The Mendelssohns' houses at 48 Markgrafenstrasse and later 7 Neue Promenade – and still more the palatial residence they would occupy at 3 Leipzigerstrasse from 1825 – quickly established themselves as a focus of Berlin's cultural and intellectual life. Indeed, the family's visitors read like a roll-call of the leading European writers, thinkers and musicians of the early nineteenth century. Among those who would become familiar household faces during Felix's boyhood were the philosopher Georg Hegel, the poet and Shakespeare translator Ludwig Tieck, the poet Heinrich Heine, Jacob Grimm (of fairytale fame), E.T.A. Hoffmann, the extraordinary Humboldt brothers Wilhelm and Alexander, and the composers Hummel, Spohr, Spontini and Weber. Visitors often commented on the Mendelssohns' familial self-sufficiency, but it was a self-sufficiency founded on a network of connections with deep and ramifying roots in German culture, past and present.

Such company was an education in itself for Felix and his siblings. By 1816, however, the seven-year-old boy had also begun his formal education at a private elementary school in Berlin. In the same year Abraham and Lea, partly at the prompting of Lea's brother Jacob, had their children quietly baptised. Felix thus acquired not only the Lutheran faith (of which he would remain a lifelong adherent) but also the additional Christian names Jacob and Ludwig as well as the supplementary surname Bartholdy, which his uncle Jacob, now the owner of the eponymous dairy farm, had adopted on his own conversion a few years earlier. Abraham and Lea were themselves baptised six years after their children, by which time the liberalising Jewish measures of the previous decade had begun to unravel. But the Mendelssohns' decision was far removed in spirit from that of their friend Heine, himself a Jewish convert, who famously described baptism as 'an entry-ticket to European culture'. Rather, it seems to have followed a lengthy process of heart-searching, the terms of which are traceable in a letter that Abraham wrote to his daughter Fanny on her confirmation:

We have educated you and your brothers and sister in the Christian faith, because it is the creed of most civilised people, and contains nothing that can lead you away from what is good, and much that guides you to love, obedience, tolerance, and resignation, even if it offered nothing but the example of its founder, understood by so few, and followed by still fewer.

There is no evidence that Felix or his siblings ever regretted their parents' decision. However, none of them welcomed the addition of the Bartholdy name, not least, perhaps, because their uncle Jacob – despite his elevation to the Prussian consulship in Rome, where he lived in the Casa Bartholdy at the top of the Spanish Steps – never quite shook off a faint aura of disreputability. Indeed, the name occasioned one of the composer's rare acts of defiance against his father's authority. When Felix was in England in 1829 Abraham noted that he appeared in certain news reports and concert programmes as 'Felix Mendelssohn' rather than 'Felix Mendelssohn Bartholdy'. The omission was in fact none of Felix's doing, but Abraham took him to task for it, admitting that he regretted keeping the name Mendelssohn at all once the family was converted. He urged his son to abandon it now in favour of plain Bartholdy. 'A Christian Mendelssohn is an impossibility...' Abraham wrote. 'There can no more be a Christian Mendelssohn than there can be a Jewish Confucius.' But Felix gently stood his ground, continuing to sign himself with both names for the remainder of his life and leaving it to posterity to shed his uncle's ambiguous legacy on his behalf.

Felix's musical education began at home, where Lea herself gave him piano lessons from an early age. In 1816, however, the family accompanied Abraham on one of his business trips to Paris to oversee French war reparations. There, demonstrating once again the Mendelssohns' unerring ability to seek out the most resonant names for German culture, Felix and Fanny took piano lessons from Marie Bigot, who ten years earlier had so impressed Beethoven by sight-reading his 'Appassionata' Sonata from the notoriously disorderly autograph manuscript that the composer had made her a present of it; they also took violin lessons from the celebrated virtuoso Pierre Baillot. (En route, in Weimar, Abraham had visited the holder of the most resonant German name of all, Johann Wolfgang von Goethe, who would soon loom large in Felix's own life.) Those who heard the siblings play (including their scandalous aunt Dorothea Schlegel) were staggered by their musicianship and performance skills. The trip and the lessons were reprised in 1817, by which time those skills had developed exponentially.

The following year Abraham took Felix out of school to continue his education at home. Perhaps not surprisingly for a son of Moses Mendelssohn, Abraham was a natural pedagogue. He was often away from Berlin on business, but even in his absence he kept a close eye on his children's progress. Something of the tone of that supervision – not lacking in affection, certainly, but by modern standards patriarchal and pedantic to the point of priggishness – can be gauged from his letters home. Typical is one in which, after addressing each of the children in turn, he directs the following paragraph to the then eight-year-old Felix:

> Mother has written that she is very satisfied with you, my dear Felix, at least up to now. I am very glad to hear it and I hope that I will find a truthful and pleasant diary (when I return). Follow my admonition: 'Be truthful and obedient.' You can't do better than that, and if you are not that you couldn't do worse. Your letters gave me much pleasure but in the second there were a few slips, which I will point out to you on my return. You have to make an effort to speak better, then you'll write better.

The programme of instruction Abraham now designed for the children was both exhaustive and exhausting. Its timetabling can have left Felix scarcely a free moment during the average day, and no doubt served to inculcate that lifelong distrust of inactivity which many have seen as contributing to his early death. (Since it involved his getting up at five in the morning, it also left him with an ability to sleep profoundly at will: several friends attested to the difficulty of waking him once he had allowed himself to doze off.) Above all, perhaps, it had the effect, questionably beneficial, of separating him from other children of his own age and thus of reinforcing the already intensely familial orientation of the Mendelssohns' mental lives.

Felix's studies focused equally on the general and the musical, the former including mathematics, history, geography, modern and classical languages, painting (in which he developed considerable skills, especially in the depiction of landscape and architecture) and even gymnastics. This rigorous regimen was initially entrusted to G.A. Stenzel, a historian from the recently founded University of Berlin, and the virtuoso pianist Ludwig Berger, who had studied under Muzio Clementi. By 1819, however, the primacy of both had been displaced by the two principal tutors who were to dominate Mendelssohn's intellectual and musical development for the next seven years. The first was the philologist Carl Wilhelm Ludwig Heyse, mainly remembered today as the father of Paul Heyse, the first German writer to win the Nobel Prize for Literature. The second was the director of Berlin's Singakademie, Carl Friedrich Zelter.

Zelter was one of the more eccentric cultural products of late-eighteenth-century Berlin. A leading figure in the city's musical life, a friend of Hegel and Schiller, and one of the few people whom Goethe admitted to intimacy in his final years, Zelter was proud of his status as a self-made man, and famous for his calculated bearishness of address. He had begun his working life as a stonemason and continued to practise the trade while acquiring a musical training in the 1780s. His teachers included Christian Friedrich Carl Fasch, the founder of the Singakademie, and the influential composition tutor Johann Philipp Kirnberger, who had been a pupil of J.S. Bach in Leipzig. He thus brought to Felix's musical instruction both a profound respect for the contrapuntal procedures of the Baroque and a no-nonsense brusqueness that served healthily to deflate any tendency to pretension in his most gifted student.

For all his bluster, Zelter was quick to recognise the extraordinary nature of those gifts. At eight years old, Felix was already transposing complex piano pieces at sight, and the following year he made his public debut as a pianist in a trio for two horns and piano by Joseph Wölfl, and as a soloist in Jan Ladislav Dussek's virtuosic 'Military' Concerto, which he apparently played from memory. By the age of ten he was spotting abstruse errors of musical grammar in the works of Bach. Goethe's daughter-in-law Ottilie was astounded by the musical precocity of Felix and Fanny when they performed at one of Zelter's dinner parties in 1819. The same year saw Felix's first dateable composition: a song presented to his father on the occasion of Abraham's forty-third birthday (though a surviving sonata for two pianos may well have been written a few weeks earlier).

The young composer's meticulously organised exercise books chart a swift upward curve, their canons, fugues and chorale exercises being increasingly interspersed with original compositions. In 1820 alone he produced around forty works, including pieces for organ, piano, violin and piano, piano trio and other chamber combinations, as well as songs, a wedding cantata, a scene for soprano and tenor accompanied by winds and strings, and a one-act Singspiel. Nor did this remarkable outpouring of music, itself written against a background of intensive general study, constitute Felix's only creative work. Astonishingly – even in a household where idleness was anathema – the eleven-year-old boy's idea of relaxation was to pen a 450-verse mock-epic in dactylic hexameters, casting his younger brother Paul as hero! Little wonder that Zelter, with gruff but genuine pride, regarded Felix as his star pupil.

The seal was set on that status in October 1821 when Zelter took the prodigy to Weimar to introduce him to Goethe. It is hard nowadays to reclaim a true sense of Goethe's centrality to the age that – in the history of German culture – bears his name. Poet, novelist, artist, philosopher, statesman, scientist, he has, in our more specialised era, no single modern counterpart. He was as productive in his output as he was comprehensive in his interests, his published works alone running to 138 volumes. At the time of Felix's visit, Goethe was in his seventies and had a forbidding reputation for aloofness. Ironically, he was no great respecter of prodigies, though several visited him, and of all the arts music was the one to which he was least naturally attuned. It is all the more remarkable, therefore, that the young Mendelssohn should have had, by all accounts, as great an impact on the elderly sage during his fortnight's stay as Goethe himself did on the twelve-year-old boy.

Fanny Mendelssohn made her brother promise to relay everything Goethe said, threatening never to speak to him again if he didn't; in a letter home from Weimar Felix provided a breathlessly circumstantial account of his first meeting with the great man:

Now listen everybody, all of you!... Professor Zelter came and said, 'Goethe is here, the old gentleman is here!' In a flash we were at the bottom of the steps – in Goethe's house. He was in the garden, and was just coming around a hedge; isn't that odd, dear Father, just the way it happened when you met him? He is very friendly, but I don't think any of his portraits look at all like him. He then inspected his interesting collection of fossils, which his son organised, and kept saying: Hm, hm, I am quite pleased: afterwards I walked around the garden with him and Prof. Zelter for another half hour. Then we sat down to eat. One would think he was fifty years old, not seventy-three. After dinner Fräulein Ulrike, Goethe's [son's] wife's sister, requested a kiss, and I did likewise. Every morning I receive a kiss from the author of Faust *and of* Werther, *and every afternoon two kisses from Goethe, friend and father. Fancy that!*

The same afternoon Felix played the piano for Goethe for more than two hours, performing fugues by Bach and improvising. In the evening, when the adults played whist before dinner, Zelter warned the boy with his usual bluntness: 'Whist means that you should keep your mouth shut'.

Four days later, Felix reported that he was still playing for Goethe daily, sometimes for up to eight hours: 'He sits down beside me and when I've finished (I improvise most of the time), I ask him for a kiss or else give him one.' The boy also passed with flying colours two trials of his abilities before invited audiences that included the Grand Duke and Duchess, the composer Johann Nepomuk Hummel (Mozart's former pupil) and a sister of the Russian Tsar. On these occasions, in addition to such exciting, if rather pointless, exercises as sight-reading a messy Beethoven manuscript, Felix improvised with demonic drive. He also performed his piano transcription of the overture to Mozart's *Marriage of Figaro* and played the piano in one of his own chamber compositions. Goethe had heard the seven-year-old Mozart play in Frankfurt and, though he had been only thirteen himself at the time, did not hesitate to pronounce Felix the superior musician. He declared to Zelter:

> *what this little man can do in extemporising and playing at sight, borders on the miraculous and I could not have believed it possible at so early an age... what your pupil already accomplishes, bears the same relation to the Mozart of that time, that the cultivated talk of a grown-up person does to the prattle of a child.*

It was a verdict resoundingly endorsed by the musicians present, though Zelter injected the commonsensical caveat that 'many began like Mozart but no one ever reached him.'

Sterile though such comparisons may ultimately be, many subsequent critics have agreed that Mendelssohn's music of the early 1820s already demonstrates greater maturity and individuality than Mozart's at the same age. A more significant comparison for their respective futures, however, might be between the two boys' lifestyles and the ambitions of their respective parents. While Mozart's father Leopold paraded his son around Europe as a prodigy, Abraham was as chary of promoting Felix's wunderkind status as Zelter was; indeed, he would need some convincing that a musical career was the right one for his son at all. Abraham resigned from his partnership in the bank shortly after Felix's return from Weimar, but even so the family had no need to supplement their income with the kind of musical circus Leopold Mozart was so adept at ringmastering. Furthermore, while the Mozarts were dependent on patronage for large-scale commissions and performances, the Mendelssohns could rely on their wealth and connections to ensure the staging of Felix's chamber and orchestral works. Even his operas were produced at home, before audiences as grand as any in the more public venues of the European concert circuit. What Felix may have lost in exposure to a wide range of musical influences – not to mention the rough and tumble of public musical life – he therefore gained in ease of access to audiences and in opportunities to hear his own music as soon as it was written. This was especially true after 1821 when the Mendelssohns instituted their regular Sunday musicales.

So what was he like, this twelve-year-old who returned from Weimar at the end of 1821 with the blessing of the pre-eminent cultural icon of his age? A drawing by his future brother-in-law Wilhelm Hensel and an oil sketch by Karl Begas both show a serious, dreamy child with a cascade of dark hair that would not disgrace a Pre-Raphaelite model. Those who met him described a boy whose liveliness could border on the

Oil sketch of Mendelssohn aged twelve, by Karl Begas, 1821

temperamental. His behaviour away from the keyboard was refreshingly normal in its pre-adolescent wilfulness, and the personal charm that would beguile interlocutors throughout his life was already much in evidence. The waspishness with which Felix despatches people and institutions in many of his letters home suggests a child as much observer as observed, but he seems to have kept this critical streak veiled outside the family circle. Socially confident and outgoing, he was already characterised by a detachment that reserved the expression of his innermost self for his nearest and dearest.

The nearest and dearest of all – at this time and arguably for the rest of their lives – was his sister Fanny, now sixteen years old. The intensity of the siblings' relationship has proved a fertile source of psychological speculation over the years. Even making due allowance for societal changes since the early nineteenth century, it is hard to read Fanny's near-hysterical letters on the eve of her marriage to Wilhelm

Mendelssohn's sister Fanny, by her husband Wilhelm Hensel, 1847

Hensel in 1829 without feeling some unease at the passionate absence of discrimination between brother and husband in her image of male companionship. Hensel himself sometimes found the communication between his wife and brother-in-law as impenetrable as a code, and the not infrequent epistolary disagreements between brother and sister have the tone and dynamics of lovers' tiffs. Whatever its emotional wellsprings, however, the bond between Felix and Fanny was unquestionably the cornerstone of both their lives. Founded on a twin-like identity of outlook on the world, it depended above all on their profoundly shared understanding of and commitment to music.

Fanny was herself a musician of remarkable powers. Indeed, her talents, both as performer and as composer, attracted at least as much wonder and admiration as her brother's. Her musical memory was as uncannily retentive as his: when she was thirteen she astonished her father by playing twenty-four of Bach's preludes by heart. However, just as Moses Mendelssohn's liberalism did not extend to allowing his daughters to marry whom they liked, so Abraham's did not admit of having a daughter pursue music beyond the level of decent social accomplishment. For him, as for most fathers of his time and background, a woman's place was in the home, or at best the salon. A letter he wrote to her from Paris in the year before Felix's Weimar trip stands, like Fanny's whole life, as painful testimony to the sacrifice of talent on the altar of convention. He declared:

> *Music might perhaps become his [Felix's] profession, while for you it can and should only be an ornament, never the root of your being and doing. We may therefore pardon him some ambition and desire to be acknowledged in a pursuit which appears very important to him, because he feels a vocation for it, while it does you credit that you have always shown yourself good and sensible in these matters; and your very joy at the praise he earns proves that you might, in his place, have merited equal approval. Remain true to these sentiments and to this line of conduct; they are feminine, and only what is truly feminine is an ornament to your sex.*

Eight years later Abraham was still urging her to do her duty, to follow 'your real calling, the only calling of a young woman – I mean the state of a housewife'. After her marriage the following year, Fanny continued to play and compose, producing in all well over 400 works, predominantly songs and piano pieces. But she hardly ever appeared on the public stage as a pianist, and only in her final months – and then against the advice of her famous brother – did she summon up the confidence to publish under her own name: the vast majority of her works remain in manuscript to this day. If a privileged background has sometimes been seen as a hindrance to Felix's development, it was infinitely more so for Fanny. There is a tragic insight into the true nature of opportunity in the London *Athenaeum's* observation, in 1838, that her talents might have been known throughout the world had she been born poor.

Fanny's involvement in her brother's creative life was as highly charged as their emotional bond, and was cherished by both as a kind of symbiosis. When Felix was thirteen Fanny wrote, with a mixture of pride and possessiveness: 'I have always been his only musical adviser, and he never writes down a thought before submitting it to my judgement. For instance, I have known his operas by heart before a note was written.' Throughout her life she remained a forthright critic of his work and hypersensitive to his opinion of hers; while for his part Mendelssohn called her his 'Cantor' and continued to solicit her comments on his compositions. As late as 1836, for example, he was urging her to send him her 'strictures' on *St Paul* 'as one colleague should write to another'.

By the time Felix returned from Weimar at the end of 1821 he was already a seasoned composer, with nearly seventy works to his name. Indeed, there are few parallels in musical history for Mendelssohn's prolificacy as a child composer, or for the dizzying pace of his progress. The works of this astonishingly productive period inevitably reflect both Zelter's tastes and his methods of instruction. The Singakademie director was no modernist. He revered Bach, Haydn and Mozart, but his respect for the Viennese Classical tradition extended only to the middle works of Beethoven (whom he met in 1819), and even here his taste ran to the conservative: the latter's now routinely disparaged 'Battle Symphony' was a particular favourite. The strict contrapuntal basis of Zelter's tuition also left its mark on much of Felix's early output. Certainly, there were some outside influences. Felix heard the premiere of Weber's opera *Der Freischütz* conducted by the composer at Berlin's new Schauspielhaus in June 1821, and the work made a deep impression on his musical imagination. Weber's visit also saw the first performance of his *Konzertstück*, Op. 79, for piano and orchestra, which would become a staple of Mendelssohn's performing repertoire and an abiding influence on his own compositions for piano and orchestra. But for the most part the works of these years map the course of Felix's studies as composer and instrumentalist, the enthusiasms instilled by his teachers, and the events of the family's crowded domestic calendar.

Thus the spirit of Mozart informs the bubbly three-movement Violin Sonata in F major of 1820, one of several pieces for violin and piano that seem to have coincided with the admission to the tutorial ranks of the Mendelssohn household of the young violin teacher Eduard Rietz. Similarly, early Beethoven seems to stand behind the Piano Sonata in G minor of 1821, especially in the searching *Adagio*, a movement of remarkable maturity for a twelve-year-old. One of six piano sonatas written in 1820 and 1821 (most of which still remain in manuscript) the Sonata in G minor was published as Op. 105 after Mendelssohn's death. On his way to see Goethe in the autumn of 1821, Felix played it in Leipzig for J.G. Schicht, one of Bach's successors as Thomaskantor. (The occasion marked Mendelssohn's first visit to the city with which his name would be indelibly associated in later years.)

The piano sonata is dated 18 August 1821. By the middle of the following month Mendelssohn had completed the first five works in a sequence of thirteen string symphonies that stand at the centre of his early output; a sixth was completed in the autumn. Virtually unknown before the 1960s, the string symphonies hark back to the earlier eighteenth century in their choice of form, style and forces. As such they belong not to the Beethovenian symphonic tradition but to the pre-Classical tradition of the three-movement Italian and German sinfonia (Mendelssohn's own designation for them). The first six symphonies all have three movements, as against the four of the Viennese Classical model, and contrapuntal textures dominate, especially in the outer movements, which are typically characterised by their unflagging rhythmic drive. Their greatest debt is owed to C.P.E. Bach, another of Zelter's musical heroes, though the Baroque is seldom far away, as for example in the use of a *siciliano* in the second movement of No. 1, and the trio sonata inflections of the second movement of No. 2. Also typical of the pre-Classical sinfonia is the absence of conventional sonata form, with its formal contrasts, as an organising principle. When the symphonies were first performed at the Mendelssohns' Sunday musicales Felix even provided a continuo part on the piano – by the 1820s a thoroughly outmoded practice.

For all their deliberate archaism, these are works of remarkable precocity. As one might expect in so young a composer, their emotional content consistently lags behind their technical proficiency, but perhaps the clearest sign of immaturity lies in their disparateness, which typically results in the total effect of each being less than the sum of its parts.

In No. 4, for example, the outer movements breathe the bracing air of the early eighteenth century – the portentous slow introduction could easily belong to a Baroque overture – while the slow movement is a yearningly Romantic *Andante*. Only in No. 6, completed shortly before Felix's departure for Weimar in October 1821, do we seem to move towards the world of Viennese Classicism. There are shades of Haydn in the unison opening and the *Prestissimo* finale, while the second movement takes the form of a minuet with two trios. The second of the trios introduces a noble chorale-like melody which prefigures Mendelssohn's use of chorales in such later works as the 'Reformation' and *Lobgesang* symphonies, and is one of few moments in the first string symphonies when the characteristic voice of the mature composer can be glimpsed without undue benefit of hindsight.

One of the most remarkable aspects of Mendelssohn's rapid creative growth in the early 1820s is the sheer range of forms and genres he essayed. As we have seen, these included opera – a medium that is almost exclusively associated with his earliest years as a composer, despite his ambitions to revisit it in later life. He had already completed his first comic opera, the French vaudeville-inspired one-act Singspiel *Die Soldatenliebschaft* ('Soldiers' Love Affairs'), by the end of 1820. Like the cantata *In rührend feierlichen Tönen*, written for the wedding of two of his cousins in June the same year, *Die Soldatenliebschaft* had its origins not in his studies with Zelter but in a family celebration. In this case the occasion was his father's forty-fourth birthday on 11 December, and Felix composed the whole work – an overture and eleven numbers – in less than ten weeks without showing it to anyone outside the immediate family. *Die Soldatenliebschaft* was duly performed on Abraham's birthday, with piano accompaniment only, and was staged again a few weeks

23

later to mark Felix's twelfth birthday in February 1821, this time before an audience of invited guests in a specially constructed theatre at the Mendelssohns' residence and with a full orchestra recruited from the ranks of the royal Kapelle. The performance was preceded by a French farce, *L'Homme automate* ('The Human Automaton'), for which Felix had also composed an overture, now lost. Lea Mendelssohn regarded this concert as the moment when her son's calling was determined, and a letter to one of her cousins gives a touchingly proud account of the occasion:

> *The ensembles reveal a knowledge of contrapuntal writing, but above all the orchestration an insight that for a first attempt borders on the incredible... It seemed to me impossible that a child could be so confident writing for each section of the orchestra – not even twenty errors occurred – and that many found his score not unplayable, when one considers that no expert had seen even one line of it, let alone retouched it... It was a uniquely lovely moment for the parents' hearts, to see their beautiful child with Raphael-like locks sitting among all the artists, his eyes always enlivened by the music, radiant and flashing with uncommon energy, and above the child's features streamed an expression of bliss and coyness.*

By now, however, Felix was already at work on a second comic opera, *Die beiden Pädagogen* ('The Two Teachers'), by the same librettist – the family friend and future professor of forensic pathology Johann Ludwig Casper whom Lea Mendelssohn rather grandly dubbed their 'house poet'. This time the writing took less than seven weeks, and *Die beiden Pädagogen* – a light-hearted Mozartian reflection on the value of education – was ready for Lea's forty-fourth birthday on 15 March. The work was performed with piano accompaniment on the big day, and Lea reported that the normally imperturbable Zelter had tears in his eyes as he turned the pages of the score.

Mendelssohn's third opera was well under way by the time of his visit to Goethe in the autumn, and was finished on 9 December, shortly after his return to Berlin. Composed to another vaudevillian Casper libretto, *Die wandernden Komödianten* ('The Travelling Players') is a one-act Singspiel about the adventures of a troupe of itinerant actors, and was staged at the Mendelssohns' residence in April, on a double-bill with *Die beiden Pädagogen*. The following month Felix turned his attention to Casper's fourth Singspiel libretto, *Die beiden Neffen*, also known as *Der Onkel aus Boston* ('The Two Nephews' or 'The Uncle from Boston'). Around the same time, his first large-scale sacred works – a *Gloria* in E flat major and a *Magnificat* in D major, both scored for solo voices, chorus and orchestra and both composed since his return from Weimar – were first heard at one of the Mendelssohns' Sunday musicales.

In July 1822 the family set off on another of their periodic travels, this time to Switzerland. Their outward journey took them to Potsdam, where Felix was accidentally left behind, only to be retrieved on the road, with a peasant girl by his side, as he enterprisingly followed the main company on foot. They also visited Kassel, where the children played and talked music with the new Kapellmeister Louis Spohr; and in Frankfurt Felix met a fellow musical prodigy, the ten-year-old Ferdinand Hiller, who would for many years be one of his closest friends. The Swiss mountains left a deep impression on him. During the course of the three-month holiday he climbed the Rigi and the Wengern Alp, visited the Grindelwald glacier and Lake Geneva, reported to Zelter on the 'beautiful... mingling or answering echoes' of the yodelling he heard in the mountains and valleys, and recorded what he saw in an entire portfolio of finely crafted drawings – a tribute both to his natural talent and to the skills of his drawing teacher, Samuel Rösel. Felix was less impressed by his exposure to Swiss folk music – he retained a lifelong suspicion of all such 'national' music – but it left its trace in two of the string symphonies he wrote the following year: the scherzo movements of Nos 9 and 11 make startling use of Swiss folk material, in the latter case incongruously supported by a battery of 'Turkish' percussion. It was on their way home from Switzerland in October that Abraham and Lea were quietly baptised in Frankfurt. Three days later the whole family paid Goethe a visit in Weimar, where they were gratified by the great man's likening his and Felix's relationship to that of Saul and David in the Book of Samuel.

On his return to Berlin Felix continued work on *Die beiden Neffen*, the first act of which he had finished in Lausanne in September. Within days of getting back he also completed the work he chose to designate his Opus 1 when it was published the following year: the Piano Quartet No. 1 in C minor. This was in fact his second essay in the form: the earlier Piano Quartet in D minor seems to have been the work he played before Goethe's assembled notables in 1821. Like Felix's first operas, the quartet is eloquent testimony to his love of Mozart, whose own piano quartets stand pre-eminent among earlier contributions to this under-represented genre. A fresh seriousness of purpose is evident from the opening bars, in which the mysterious first theme is introduced by the cello. Just as Fanny commented on the new virility of Felix's appearance at this time, so the four-movement quartet sounds like the work of a young man now keenly conscious of his responsibility to the expectations of others (comparisons with the young Mozart were already becoming common currency among Berlin's intellectual elite). Indeed, the whole work is notably more Mozartian than anything he had written before. Only the slightly louche second subject of the first movement speaks unequivocally of the 1820s, though the third movement can be heard as a precursor, at several removes, of the characteristic 'elfin' mode of the mature Mendelssohn scherzo.

Mozart presides, too, over the Mendelssohn's String Symphony No. 8, also written in the closing months of 1822. With this, one of his most ambitious and powerful works to date, Mendelssohn moves firmly into the world of late-eighteenth-century Vienna. In particular, the last movement stands as an act of competitive homage to the stupendous contrapuntal finale of Mozart's 'Jupiter' Symphony, a perennial source of wonder and admiration for Mendelssohn. It is indicative of the special place the Eighth String Symphony held in his development that he immediately rescored it for full orchestra, in which form it seems to have been performed at a public concert in Berlin the following April by the court orchestra.

The other big works of 1822, a pair of concertos for solo instrument and strings, scale somewhat lesser heights than the Piano Quartet No. 1 and the String Symphony No. 8. On 5 December Felix gave the first public performance of his Piano Concerto in A minor. If the inspiration for this work was Hummel's Op. 85 Piano Concerto in the same key, which Fanny seems to have performed at one of the Mendelssohns' musicales earlier in the year, the Violin Concerto in D minor represents an unexpected return to the model of C.P.E. Bach. The latter work was written for Eduard Rietz, who had graduated from teacher to firm friend, and is Mendelssohn's first venture in the form that would produce, in the Violin Concerto in E minor of 1844, one of the greatest works of its kind. There is little here, however, to presage that magnificent achievement, beyond the fact that in the slow movement the cadenza precedes the recapitulation, as it famously does in the first movement of the later concerto.

Felix's travels in 1823 were limited to accompanying Abraham on a trip to Silesia in the summer to inaugurate a new furnace at his brother Nathan's iron smelter in Bad Reinerz (where, in the industrial equivalent of *noblesse oblige*, Felix treated his uncle's workforce to a concert). Indeed, his educational and musical schedule can have left little time for pursuits other than study and composition. As Zelter reported to Goethe, it was another year of giant musical strides for his young pupil. Nearly thirty compositions flowed from Felix's pen, including works for piano and organ (which he had been studying for more than two years), solo songs, substantial works of chamber music, two double concertos, the last five string symphonies, a Kyrie for solo voices and double chorus, and a fully fledged opera.

In March he completed – in just eleven days – his first string quartet, in E flat major, an assured work in which Haydn seems to jostle Mozart for supremacy, especially in the genial minuet and trio, and which concludes with a weighty fugal finale (Felix's several previous works for string quartet were all stand-alone fugues). The same month saw the composition of the Ninth String Symphony, with its excursion into Swiss folksong; and in May Felix completed an expansive Concerto for violin, piano and strings in D minor, a work far closer to the 1820s in its idiom than the Violin Concerto of the previous year, especially in the limpid lyricism of its slow movement. He performed the concerto, with Rietz taking the violin part, at the Schauspielhaus in July – one of three public appearances during the year that testify to his heightening profile in Berlin. Nine days later he dated the autograph of the five-movement String Symphony No. 11, the *Adagio* introduction of which seems at moments to foreshadow the sonorities of *The Hebrides* overture.

Meanwhile, in June, Felix had completed the Sonata in F minor for violin and piano, which he would publish in 1824 as his Opus 4. The work reveals the growing influence of Beethoven in Mendelssohn's creative life at this time, an influence which can also be felt in the last string symphonies and in the second double concerto of 1823, the Concerto in E major for two pianos, dated 17 October. Indeed, the influence is so strong in the first movement of the sonata that it seems at times on the verge of metamorphosing into Beethoven's 'Tempest' Sonata, Op. 31 No. 2. Similarly in the concerto, which Felix and Fanny performed at 7 Neue Promenade in December, the entry of the pianos in the first movement is conspicuously indebted to the opening pages of Beethoven's 'Emperor' Concerto, a debt not wholly discharged in the remainder of the movement. Additional wind and timpani parts have survived for the Concerto for violin, piano and strings, perhaps intended for the Schauspielhaus performance, but the Double Piano Concerto is Mendelssohn's first concerto to be scored *ab initio* for full orchestra.

Four days before the siblings gave the first performance of the Double Concerto Felix had completed the Piano Quartet in F minor, Op. 2, another work that bears the mark of his immersion in middle-period Beethoven. Dedicated to Zelter, it was the second of the three piano quartets that would introduce Mendelssohn to the musical world as a published composer. The quartet's first movement has atmospheric and thematic links with a sonata movement for piano in B flat minor which Felix dated the previous week, and the flowing third movement, which stands in for the expected scherzo, is the first in his oeuvre to be designated 'Intermezzo'. Three weeks later, on 29 December, he laid down his pen on his thirteenth and last string symphony, a single fugal movement often known simply as the *Sinfoniesatz* in C minor.

The end of the year also saw the completion of the comic opera *Die beiden Neffen*, Mendelssohn's last collaboration with Casper, which he had been working on since May 1822. As such a relatively long gestation suggests, this was a more substantial work than its one-act predecessors. Its three acts tell the story of two nephews who return to Germany from America after the Revolution, and while the dramatic pace may flag, *Die beiden Neffen* contains some sparkling music, including the delightful ballet in Act 2 and the Act 3 chain-finale. The opera was staged twice at the Mendelssohns' residence as part of the celebrations for Felix's fifteenth birthday in February 1824, the orchestra being drawn once more from the royal Kapelle. Rehearsals were held on the birthday itself, and Zelter marked the occasion by a speech in which, with Masonic ceremony, he declared Felix 'an independent fellow of the fraternity of musicians; this in the name of Mozart, Haydn, and old father Bach' and exhorted him to 'work on until you become a master'. It was, in a sense, the formal end of Felix's apprenticeship, though Zelter continued to give him lessons until 1826. In 1829 the pupil would pay grateful tribute to his old teacher for having instructed him 'not according to rigid, constricting theorems, but in true freedom, i.e., in the knowledge of proper boundaries'.

Felix's fifteenth birthday was also the probable occasion of a gift which would come to bear enormous significance both in his own career and in the wider history of music. The provenance and timing of this gift have been the source of much discussion, but it seems to have been here that his maternal grandmother, Bella Salomon, presented him with a score of Bach's *St Matthew Passion*, probably based indirectly on Bach's autograph parts. Zelter, one of few musicians to interest himself in Bach's choral music in the early years of the nineteenth century, kept his own collection of Bach scores under lock and key (including a manuscript of the *Passion* apocryphally said to have been bought from a cheese merchant who had used it as wrapping paper!), and even his prodigious pupil was denied access to them. Mendelssohn had long yearned to investigate this musical Aladdin's cave, and having a score of the *Passion* to himself was the fulfilment of a dream. It was also the first step towards his groundbreaking revival of the work five years later.

At the end of March 1824 Felix completed a composition which, having left the *Sinfoniesatz* as a torso a few months earlier, he conceived as his thirteenth symphony. The Symphony No. 1 in C minor, as it is known to posterity, was his first to be written for full orchestra. It shares a key with its unfinished predecessor, but little else. One of only three symphonies Mendelssohn allowed to be published during his lifetime (as Op. 11), the work decisively embraces the Beethovenian symphonic model. Its debt to the latter's great Symphony No. 5, however, is more a matter of key and formal structure than of spirit. Despite its minor tonality, this is a work of youthful zest and vibrancy in which, even if some of its accents are borrowed, the musical voice is recognisably that of the mature Mendelssohn. The characteristic contrapuntal textures of the earlier sinfonias, with their echoes of the schoolroom, are almost entirely absent. The third movement, a scherzo in all but name, adapts the minuet of Felix's recently composed Sonata for viola and piano in C minor, and contains the symphony's most conspicuous reference to Beethoven's Fifth in the eerie transition from trio back to minuet. The movement was in turn replaced by an orchestration of the scherzo from the Octet when the symphony was performed to resounding acclaim in London during Mendelssohn's visit of 1829.

In April Mendelssohn composed a *Salve regina* in E flat major for soprano and strings and a Sonata in the same key for clarinet and piano. The following month saw the completion of the Piano Sextet in D major, Op. 110, scored for the unusual combination of piano, violin, two violas, cello and double bass. The sextet's outer movements are among the most carefree of Mendelssohn's youthful creations, and such shadows as there are in the slow second movement seem cast only by summer clouds. The *Menuetto* that follows threatens mischief, but even its return in the closing pages of the finale (another experiment with its origins in Beethoven's Symphony No. 5) cannot unsettle the work's indomitably sunny atmosphere.

Mendelssohn's first concert overture – a form he was to make distinctively his own – also belongs to the summer of 1824. In July Felix and Abraham visited the resort of Bad Doberan, where the composer, as well as having his first dip in the sea, was fascinated by the town's wind band. With its forces in mind, he composed a *Harmoniemusik* in C major for eleven wind instruments, a work which, revised two years later, found its published form in 1839 as the *Overture for Harmoniemusik*, Op. 24.

In November Felix completed the second of his concertos for two pianos. Conceived as a concert work for himself and Fanny to play, the Concerto in A flat major is on a larger scale even than its E major predecessor. As in the Symphony No. 1, Beethoven is a pervasive influence, and the massive opening movement makes unashamed use of the Fifth Symphony's signature rhythm; but Mendelssohn's grasp is precociously secure, and here, as in the luminous slow movement and almost Chopinesque finale that follow, it is easy to forget that the concerto is the work of a boy not yet sixteen years old.

Despite such creative advances, in the closing months of 1824 the question of Felix's future remained open. Abraham in particular continued to harbour doubts about the suitability of a musical career. Was it secure? Was it a respectable choice for an offspring of the Mendelssohns? It is a striking confirmation of Lea's description of her husband as a 'skilled worrier' that Abraham even had doubts as to whether Felix was sufficiently gifted. He seems to have lost no opportunity of raising the question with the professional musicians he ran across at this time. While Felix was in the final stages of writing his Double Concerto in A flat major, the composer and piano virtuoso Ignaz Moscheles paid a six-week visit to Berlin and soon found his way to the Mendelssohns' residence. Moscheles's diary records his astonishment at the attainments of Felix and Fanny, but also at the fact that Abraham and Lea could entertain a shred of doubt about their eldest son's vocation:

> *This is a family the like of which I have never known. Felix, a boy of fifteen, is a phenomenon. What are all prodigies as compared with him? Gifted children, but nothing else. This Felix Mendelssohn is already a mature artist... Both parents are far from overrating their children's talents; in fact, they are anxious about Felix's future, and to know whether his gift will prove sufficient to lead to a noble and truly great career. Will he not, like so many other brilliant children, suddenly collapse? I asserted my conscientious conviction that Felix would ultimately become a great master, that I had not the slightest doubt of his genius; but again and again I had to insist on my opinion, before they believed me.*

Moscheles was bowled over when he heard the siblings perform Felix's Double Concerto in E major one Sunday; he also attended a concert that included the Symphony No. 1 in C minor. Unsurprisingly, therefore, he took some persuading before he would agree to give Felix piano lessons, and even then insisted that in truth it was Felix who was the master.

But the decisive opinion was not to be that of Moscheles. In March 1825 Mendelssohn accompanied his father on one of his periodic trips to Paris. Five months earlier Fanny Sebastiani had made her disastrous ducal marriage, thus rendering redundant her long-suffering governess Henriette Mendelssohn, and Abraham was to accompany his sister back to Berlin from the French capital. While he was there he took the opportunity to ask the grand old man of the French musical scene, Luigi Cherubini, the same question he had been asking his musical visitors for months. Was his son cut out for music?

Cherubini was a notoriously reserved figure. Then sixty-five, his glory days as a composer were behind him, but they had endowed him with the daunting status of an institution. As director of the Paris Conservatoire, his good opinion was sought by many but gained by few. The young Mendelssohn proved one of very few indeed to receive not just approval but, by Cherubini's taciturn standards, fulsome public endorsement. As Felix wrote home on 6 April:

> *Everyone who knows him is amazed that after he heard my F minor quartet [Op. 2], performed most miserably, he came up to me smiling and nodded to me. Then he told the others: 'Ce garçon est riche, il fera bien; il fait même déjà bien; mais il dépense trop de son argent, il met trop d'étoffe dans son habit.' ['This boy is rich, he will do well; he is already*

doing well; but he spends too much of his money, he puts
too much material in his clothes.'] Everyone declared that
this was unheard of...

Keen to test the young man's abilities further, Cherubini set
Felix to compose a Kyrie for five-part choir and orchestra,
which the latter completed by 6 May with sufficient
distinction for Cherubini to offer to take him on as a pupil.
The offer was declined, but Cherubini's faith in Felix removed
Abraham's last remaining doubts about the suitability of a
musical career.

Paris was not all music for Mendelssohn. He marvelled at
the size and pace of the metropolis, admired the brightness of
the new-fangled gas lighting and engaged in a frenetic round
of social calls. Those who had met him before commented on
how much he had changed. No longer the flowing-haired boy
perpetually on the verge of mischief, he was now a gracious
adept of the salon and the drawing-room. Had they been
party to his letters home, they would have known that he
was also a sharp – not to say bumptious – critic of Parisian
cultural life. He spared neither people nor practices, reporting
with contempt how 'when music is being played the ladies tell
each other fairytales, or jump from one chair to the next as if
they were playing musical chairs', and how he had fixed one
offender with a fierce stare from the keyboard when her noisy
fanning disturbed his performance. He was dismissive of the
orchestras, not least for regarding Beethoven's Symphony
No. 2, then more than twenty years old, as a concert novelty.
Having gone out of his way to hear the celebrated diva
Giuditta Pasta, he wrote with donnish disappointment: 'Her
voice is raw and unclear, and her intonation is not clean, and
so far I haven't been able to overlook these two faults.' Few of
the established names of the French musical scene escaped

unscathed. Meyerbeer was a figure of fun, whose disquisition on the French horn caused him, or so he claimed, almost to fall off his chair with laughter. Sigismund Neukomm, a composer of wide experience and even wider travels, was dubbed 'Altkomm' for his learned fuguing; and Anton Reicha, Cherubini's erudite colleague at the Conservatoire, was written off as a 'wild huntsman (he hunts parallel fifths)' – a pursuit hardly unknown to Felix himself. Rossini, whose works were the toast of the Théâtre-Italien, and to whom the young composer was introduced at an evening salon, was 'the great Maestro Windbag'. 'He has a puzzling face,' Felix reported to his mother. 'A mixture of roguishness, superficiality, and ennui, with long sideburns, wide as a church door, elegantly dressed, surrounded by all the ladies, answering their attempts to entertain him only rarely with a little smile.' Nor did he spare his own contemporaries. The fourteen-year-old Liszt, one of a phalanx of piano virtuosos then astonishing audiences in the French capital, had 'many fingers, but little brains.' Even Cherubini was not immune from Felix's barbs. 'He is dried up and wizened,' he wrote after the very concert at which the old man had given him his blessing. 'The other day I heard one of his masses at the royal chapel, and it was as droll as he is peevish, i.e. beyond all measure.' He was, Felix wrote, an extinct volcano that 'occasionally spews forth, but is covered with ashes and stones.'

All good knockabout stuff, and Mendelssohn would revise most of these judgements in the years to come. But it is hard not to suspect a degree of insecurity behind the sheer comprehensiveness of the broadside, as if the letters home served to some extent as a safety valve for the self-doubt he seldom showed before strangers but which was always to be a part of his creative make-up. Paris was, after all, at the very centre of European musical life, and many of the musicians he met there were international celebrities. Felix, on the other hand, was still, for all his polish, a child of the private salon; his was as yet a sheltered talent. Even Fanny felt moved to protest that he was going too far in his criticisms. But her brother had the bit between his teeth. If her irritation was in part a reaction to hearing him cavil at a feast from which she was excluded, Felix's response must have rubbed salt in the wound. 'Just consider, I beseech you,' he wrote in reply to her gentle reprimand, 'are you in Paris or am I? Surely I must know more about it than you.'

Felix and Abraham spent more than seven weeks in the French capital. They broke both the outward and the return journey at Weimar for the by now traditional visit to Goethe, and it was there, on their way back to Berlin on 20 May, that Felix performed his latest chamber work before the man to whom it was dedicated. Written in January, the Piano Quartet in B minor, Op. 3, is the last and most powerful of the three piano quartets published by the composer, and perhaps his most fully formed work before the breakthrough Octet later the same year. The outer movements in particular evince a brooding intensity new to Felix's musical language, while in the equally restless third movement the characteristic Mendelssohn scherzo comes of age. There is more than a little of the witches' sabbath about this windswept *perpetuum mobile*, an atmosphere on which Goethe – whose appreciation of music was always keener if he could find a visual correlative for it – later remarked to his companion and secretary Johann Peter Eckermann. The scherzo had 'character', he said. 'This eternal whirling and turning brought to my imagination the witches' dances on the Blocksberg, and thus I had a concept after all to associate with this wondrous music.'

Felix's career prospects were not the only change in the air on his return from Paris at the end of May. The previous year, Abraham and Lea had begun looking for a new property in Berlin, and their choice had alighted on a palatial mansion in Leipzigerstrasse, formerly the home of an impoverished nobleman. By the summer of 1825 a costly programme of refurbishment was sufficiently advanced for parts of the house to be ready for occupation. The move represented the most significant change in the Mendelssohns' material circumstances since their nocturnal flight from Hamburg fourteen years earlier. Within weeks it was to be matched by an equally spectacular change in Felix's creative life. For it was here, in the opulent surroundings of an estate to which he would return time and again in later life, that in October 1825 the sixteen-year-old composer made what Sir George Grove aptly described as his 'wonderful leap into maturity'.

Chapter 2

The Leap into Maturity (1825–1829)

"

By the summer of 1825 he was regarded by many of those who knew him as a miracle of nature…

"

The Leap into Maturity (1825–1829)

Number 3 Leipzigerstrasse was one of the grandest of the Prussian capital's grand houses. Situated near the Potsdam Gate in one of the most fashionable areas of the city, it provided a luxurious focus for the family's unflagging social and cultural activities. It was a house that hid its light under a bushel. The range facing the street was disproportionately long and shallow, but behind it a courtyard was enclosed by two extensive wings and a nineteen-room garden house (Gartenhaus). The latter overlooked several acres of garden stretching down to meadows and a farmstead from which the family drew their dairy supplies. While the rest of the house was being rescued from the dilapidation into which it had fallen, the Mendelssohns lived in the Gartenhaus, the seclusion of which muted the bustle of the city and furnished them with a passable simulacrum of country living. It is tempting to see this extraordinary new residence as symbolic of the Mendelssohns' self-imposed semi-detachment. As converted Jews in an increasingly nationalistic German climate, they were at once of and separate from Berlin high society. Like 3 Leipzigerstrasse itself, they presented an imposing façade to the world, but their real life went on behind it, inward looking, private and sheltered.

According to Fanny's son, Sebastian Hensel, the early years at Leipzigerstrasse were among the family's happiest

Mendelssohn's own drawing of the Gartenhaus in Leipzigerstrasse

times together. Based on his mother's memories, Hensel's roseate account portrays a kind of enchanted domestic world, in which the young siblings 'led a fantastic, dreamlike life'. It was a world 'full of poetry, music, merry games, ingenious practical jokes, disguises and representations'. The children even produced their own cod-literary journals, the *Garden Times* and its successor the *Tea and Snow Journal*, to the pages of which Abraham would confide his well-known wistful self-description as a kind of human hyphen between a famous father and a famous son.

It was a world, too, that drew in a widening circle of friends and visitors from across the continent. To this period belong the regular visits of men such as Hegel, Heine, and the polymathic explorer and scientist Alexander von Humboldt. It was also a time when Mendelssohn forged or consolidated some of the most important friendships of his life: with the actor and singer Eduard Devrient, the diplomat Karl Klingemann, the violinist Ferdinand David, and the controversial journalist and music theorist Adolf Bernhard Marx (known to the family as the 'Abbé', after his initials). But, as the theologian and close family friend Julius Schubring observed, there were many less distinguished visitors too. His description of the Mendelssohn ménage around this time neatly captures its dichotomously private–public nature:

Their existence was a domestic one, inasmuch as they felt little inclination to go out, being most partial, after the labours of the day, to spending the evening in familiar intercourse with one another. It was seldom, however, that they were found quite alone; they either had a number of young people who were on a friendly footing with them, or else their circle was filled up with another class of visitors. Whoever felt inclined went, and whoever took a pleasure in going was welcome. Science, art, and literature were equally represented… Celebrated and uncelebrated people, travellers of all kinds, and especially musicians, though not to the exclusion of other artists, found their efforts judiciously appreciated. The conversation was always animated and spirited.

This charmed circle revolved increasingly around Felix himself. By the summer of 1825 he was regarded by many of those who knew him as a miracle of nature, his musical gifts enhanced by personal charm and all the social and intellectual accomplishments instilled by his extraordinary background and education. At the age of sixteen he already had some 130 compositions to his name. In July he wrote what would become his fifth published work, the Capriccio in F sharp minor for piano, Op. 5 – a virtuosic exploration of the possibilities opened up by the *perpetuum mobile* mode of the scherzo in the Third Piano Quartet. The following month saw the completion of his fifth opera, *Die Hochzeit des Camacho* ('Camacho's Wedding'), Op. 10, a treatment of an episode in the second volume of Cervantes' *Don Quixote* on which he had been working since June 1824. The pastor who confirmed Felix in the Protestant faith in September 1825 chose well when he took as his text a passage from Luke 12:48: 'For unto whomsoever much is given, of him shall be much required.'

High expectations indeed, but they were to be fulfilled sooner than anyone present at the confirmation could possibly have anticipated. For nothing in Mendelssohn's vast portfolio of compositions (or in anyone else's *oeuvre*, for that matter) prepared his friends and family for the breakthrough he was to make the following month. On 15 October 1825 – coincidentally the very day Beethoven moved to his final lodgings in Vienna – Felix dated the work that would propel him into the front rank of contemporary composers. The

Octet in E flat major, Op. 20 is unique in musical history. Its irresistible verve, buttressed by the highest craftsmanship, would have earned it a leading place in the canon of classical music regardless of the circumstances of its composition. As the work of a sixteen-year-old its assurance and originality are astounding. Never before or since has a composer achieved maturity so completely and decisively in a single work. Even its form is without precedent. Spohr had written the first of his double string quartets, but, as he himself observed, he had never aimed at providing the eight performers with the degree of independence that the younger composer had invested in his. Here the intense compositional experience of the past seven years is translated into a language entirely Mendelssohn's own. The first movement's exhilarating breadth of compass is wholly characteristic of the mature composer, while the ensuing *Andante*, with its deliberate, at times almost Corellian, archaisms, is one of his most profoundly felt slow movements. Mendelssohn's signature is equally unmistakable in the scurrying texture of the scherzo, marked *Allegro leggierissimo*. The concluding *Presto* – another tribute to the Mozart of the 'Jupiter' finale – deploys Felix's formidable battery of contrapuntal skills while never sacrificing accessibility to learning. Mendelssohn's grip here is so secure that he is able to conflate heterogeneous elements without any sense of incongruity: the first subject, for example, takes the form of an eight-part fugue; a transitional subject emerges in the development as a theme derived from Handel's *Messiah* ('And he shall reign for ever and ever'); and the movement incorporates references to the scherzo with an organic inevitability that was still eluding Mendelssohn only a few months earlier when he used a similar device in the finale of the Third Piano Quartet. When the Octet was published in 1832 the composer specified that it should be 'played by all the instruments in the style of a symphony' and there is no mistaking the symphonic nature of its sweep and ambition. For Mendelssohn himself, as he told his friend Robert Schumann many years later, the work became a happy reminder of his youth, and he always kept a special place for it in his musical affections.

The Octet was dedicated to Eduard Rietz, whose twenty-third birthday fell two days after its completion and for whom the virtuosic first violin part was evidently designed. Beyond that, its origins are hidden in what, for this most self-documenting of families, amounts to radio silence. Fanny did reveal, however, that a germ of the work lay in her brother's reading of Goethe's *Faust*. In particular, Felix confided to her that in the scherzo he had set to music the final stanza of the Walpurgisnacht dream sequence in Part 1 of the celebrated poem:

Wolkenzug und Nebelflor
erhellen sich von oben.
Luft im Laub und Wind im Rohr,
und alles ist zerstoben.

Drifting clouds and veiled mist
illumined from above.
Breeze in leaves and wind in reeds,
and everything has vanished.

'To me alone he told this idea,' she recalled, with her characteristic air of guardian of the gate:

the whole piece is to be played staccato *and* pianissimo, *the tremulandos [sic] coming in now and then, the trills passing away with the quickness of lightning; everything new and strange, and at the same time most insinuating and pleasing, one feels so near the world of spirits, carried away in the air, half inclined to snatch up a broomstick and follow the aerial procession. At the end the first violin takes a flight with a feather-like lightness and – everything has vanished.*

This is wholly true to the evanescent spirit of the scherzo. It also suggests a quasi-programmatic element for at least part of the Octet, and as such points ahead to other works in which extra-musical sources of inspiration would become increasingly important to Mendelssohn. Since the Walpurgisnacht dream episode in *Faust* is subtitled 'the golden wedding of Oberon and Titania', Fanny's account hints, too, that the seeds of the next, and equally breathtaking, major work of Mendelssohn's maturity – the following summer's overture to *A Midsummer Night's Dream* – may already have been planted by the time he completed the Octet in October 1825.

As if giving the nineteenth century one of its finest works of chamber music were not achievement enough, on the very same day that he finished the Octet Felix marked his tutor Heyse's birthday by presenting him with a German verse translation that he had been making (in his spare time!) of Terence's Latin comedy *Andria* ('The Woman of Andros'). Heyse published the play the following year, letting it be known that the anonymous translator was gifted 'in the other Muses', and Felix sent a copy to Goethe, who was sufficiently impressed to regale his guests with readings from it. The translation would serve as Mendelssohn's entry ticket to the University of Berlin in 1827.

1826 began with a trio of short piano pieces – a Fugue in C sharp minor, a Vivace in C minor, and an Andante and Canon in D major – which served as curtain-raisers for the much more significant keyboard work Mendelssohn completed on 22 March: the Piano Sonata in E major, Op. 6. This sonata is the first composition to reveal Felix's growing interest in the music of Beethoven's last period. Indeed, it seems openly constructed on the footprint of Beethoven's Sonata in A major, Op. 101 of 1816, with which it shares aspects of form and atmosphere. Beethoven's example here seems to spur Mendelssohn to a degree of conspicuous innovation not usually considered his characteristic territory. The slow movement, with its unsettling alternation of *adagio* recitative and songlike *andante*, is particularly experimental. As in Beethoven's sonata, the runaway finale follows directly from the slow movement and incorporates references to the opening movement; Mendelssohn's voice is perhaps most immediately recognisable in the second movement (a species of elfin minuet). For all that one can sense Beethoven looking over Felix's shoulder as he writes, however, this remains clearly the work of the composer of the Octet, and is the only piano sonata Mendelssohn saw fit to publish.

Less characteristic in this sense, ironically, is another keyboard work of 1826, the *Seven Characteristic Pieces* (*Sieben Charakterstücke*) for piano, Op. 7. The work was completed during the summer, though at least one of the pieces dates from two years earlier. The nebulous Germanic term *Charakterstück* can imply an element of pastiche, or at least of *hommage*, and these seven pieces are protean almost to the point of ventriloquism. Four are decidedly historical in tone: the first could almost be a Bach prelude, while the second confirms Rossini's astute observation that Mendelssohn's piano music owes something to Domenico Scarlatti; the third piece too evokes the Baroque, while the fifth – the work's centre of gravity – is one of Mendelssohn's most austerely Bachian fugues. Even the drooping melancholy of the sixth piece, ostensibly in a more modern idiom, strikes echoes of the Baroque sarabande. Only the fourth and seventh pieces have both feet planted in their time, the latter a fleeting Mendelssohnian scherzo that breathes the same air as the soon-to-be-composed *A Midsummer Night's Dream* overture. Their very eclecticism, however, makes the *Seven Pieces* characteristic in an unintended sense. In their stylistic discontinuity, their tendency to juxtapose rather than to assimilate the historical and the contemporary, they are emblematic not just of Mendelssohn's development as a composer but of an aspect of his creative personality that has sometimes sidelined him from linear readings of musical history in general. It is the same tendency, for example, that in December 1826 – only four months after the completion of the wholly original *A Midsummer Night's Dream* overture – gives us the powerful but unashamedly archaic *Te Deum* in D major for solo voices, double chorus and continuo. Written for the Singakademie, which had just moved into new purpose-built premises off Unter den Linden, the *Te Deum* looks no later than the eighteenth century for its sources of inspiration, though the ethereal fourth number, 'Tibi cherubim', transports us even further back, to the echoic seventeenth-century antiphony of St Mark's, Venice. When Lea Mendelssohn dismissed this and similarly historicist works among her son's sacred compositions as 'stillborn children', she thus unwittingly placed herself at the head of a critical tradition.

Nine days after he dated the Piano Sonata in E major Mendelssohn completed the expansive String Quintet in A major, Op. 18 for two violins, two violas and cello. Here the continuities with the Octet are far more obvious. The unforgettably bittersweet final theme of the first movement's exposition, for example, clearly occupies the same magical world as the scherzo of the Octet and prepares the ground for another scurryingly supernatural scherzo in the Quintet itself. When the Quintet was published in 1833, Mendelssohn replaced the minuet (which had originally formed the work's second movement) with a sober Intermezzo in memory of his friend Eduard Rietz, who had died the previous year.

Also completed in March 1826 was the 'Trumpet' Overture, so called after the fanfares that punctuate its sonata form. Just as the Quintet would no doubt loom larger in the Mendelssohn canon were it not for the Octet, so the 'Trumpet' Overture has never escaped the shadow of the much greater concert overture with which he would crown his year's work a few months later. Seldom performed today, it was apparently Abraham's favourite among his son's compositions. Felix himself dusted it off at least three times – first for the Dürer tercentenary celebrations in Berlin in 1828, then for a festival performance in Düsseldorf in 1833, and again for a Philharmonic concert in London the same year – but he never published it. Not until twenty years after his death did it appear as his Op. 101.

On 7 July 1826 Felix wrote to Fanny telling her that he was about 'to dream the *Midsummer Night's Dream*' and was wondering at his own audacity. It is the first surviving mention of one of the most enduringly popular works in classical music and the second composition of Mendelssohn's youth to which that much-overworked term 'masterpiece' can be justly applied. *A Midsummer Night's Dream* (*Ein* *Sommernachtstraum*), Op. 21 has its origins in the composer's recent reading of Shakespeare's plays in the enormously influential German translations of August Wilhelm Schlegel (the brother of aunt Dorothea's husband Friedrich). But the music seems also to partake of the Mendelssohns' domestic entertainments during that magical summer of 1826, which passed, according to Sebastian Hensel, 'like one uninterrupted festival day'. The four ethereal wind chords that begin the overture lift the veil on an enchanted world. The 'fairy' music that follows picks up where the scherzo of the Octet left off, weaving a gossamer web around a succession of themes emblematic of Theseus' courtiers, the wandering lovers and the 'rude mechanicals', the latter complete with the brays of the metamorphosed Bottom. The chords return at the beginning of the recapitulation and also – following a passage of breathtaking beauty in which time itself seems suspended – at the very end of the overture, as if lowering the curtain once more after our privileged glimpse into fairyland.

With *A Midsummer Night's Dream*, Mendelssohn gave definition to the nascent genre of the concert overture, which was to inspire some of his finest works over the coming years. While not strictly programmatic, it nevertheless marks a significant step towards the embodiment of extra-musical ideas in musical form represented by such later works as *The Hebrides* and *Calm Sea and Prosperous Voyage* overtures and the 'Italian' and 'Scottish' symphonies. Above all, it is music of a freshness that continues to speak directly to each new generation. Even George Bernard Shaw – no great lover of Mendelssohn's music – remarked of *A Midsummer Night's Dream* that it affords history's 'most striking example of a very young composer astonishing the world by a musical style at once fascinating, original and perfectly new... One can actually feel the novelty now, after sixty-six years'. More than a century has passed since Shaw's review, but the overture remains as pristine as ever.

A Midsummer Night's Dream was given its first airing in a piano duet performance by Felix and Fanny at Leipzigerstrasse in November. The audience included Moscheles, who was back in Berlin for another concert tour and was amazed at how far Felix had advanced in the year since he had last seen him. Not until February 1827, however, did the overture receive its first public orchestral performance, at a concert in Stettin (Szczecin) that also featured Mendelssohn's Double Piano Concerto in A flat major, with the composer at one of the keyboards. The occasion found Mendelssohn in exalted company, since the programme included another significant premiere – the first performance in northern Europe of Beethoven's Ninth Symphony (Felix himself played among the violins). During the same visit he privately performed (from memory) Beethoven's late 'Hammerklavier'

Sonata, Op. 106, a copy of which Karl Klingemann had given *Mendelssohn's*
Fanny as a twentieth birthday present at the end of 1825. *friend Karl*

Two months after his return from Stettin, Mendelssohn's *Klingemann, by*
opera *Die Hochzeit des Camacho* finally appeared on the *Wilhelm Hensel,*
public stage. The performance had been a long time coming. *1835*
Felix had submitted the work to the theatre management
soon after its completion in August 1825, and while he had
been working on *A Midsummer Night's Dream* in July 1826
he had had a meeting with Spontini, the notoriously prickly
musical director of the Berlin Schauspielhaus, to talk about
mounting it. The Italian had loftily demanded changes to
the score, complaining about its paucity of what he called
'grand ideas' and thereby provoking a blazing row with
Abraham. Only on 29 April 1827 did *Camacho* struggle free
of the bureaucracy and factionalism of Berlin musical life
(not to mention the last-minute illness of one of the singers)

to find its way onto the boards of the Schauspielhaus. It soon became apparent, however, that the performance was as unconvincing as the libretto, and Mendelssohn (in by no means his last such show of impetuous sensitivity) slipped out of the theatre before the end. The audience was polite enough – it was largely made up of family friends and well-wishers – but the critical reception was cool and streaked with anti-Semitism. Especially painful must have been a suggestion that the whole enterprise owed more to the Mendelssohns' wealth than to the quality of the music. Even the scrupulously loyal Devrient had mixed feelings about the opera (the more so, no doubt, for having had to cover for his friend's absence at the end). Earlier in the year, Felix had written to the Swedish composer Adolf Fredrik Lindblad, magisterially enough given that Lindblad was eight years his senior:

> Test yourself always, but after so doing be firm and resolved; allow praise and criticism (I beg you) to have only the value to you that they should have, namely that of an opinion.

After the *Camacho* premiere Felix proved unequal to his own advice. Unused as he was to public rebuff, his humiliation ran deep. A planned second performance was cancelled, and *Camacho* was never revived during his lifetime (and has hardly been heard since). What's more, the experience seems to have left him with a profound ambivalence towards the whole business of operatic composition. On the one hand, he wanted more urgently than ever to produce a successful opera; on the other, he developed a near-phobic caution towards the librettos he was offered. He would consider at least fifty potential opera projects over the coming years, but while he would write other dramatic works (including the crowning glory of his theatrical writing, the 1843 incidental music for *A Midsummer Night's Dream*), his first foray onto the public opera stage would also be his last.

It was not only in his musical life that Mendelssohn, at the age of eighteen, was beginning to emerge from the domestic cocoon of Leipzigerstrasse. Higher musicianship and higher education seldom went hand in hand in the early nineteenth century, but Abraham and Lea were determined that Felix should prove an exception in this respect as in so many others: in May 1827, after nine years of the most intensive private tuition, Mendelssohn matriculated at the University of Berlin, where he would study for the next two years. Even here, however, he would be among familiar faces. Several of the teaching staff were family friends, including Eduard Gans (the legal authority and later suitor to Felix's younger sister Rebecka) and Alexander von Humboldt, some of whose research on the earth's magnetic field was conducted from the Mendelssohns' garden. Felix also attended Hegel's celebrated lectures on aesthetics, the influence of which on the young composer has been much debated.

It was in May 1827, too, that Felix composed his last piano sonata. Beethoven had died in Vienna in March and it seems likely that the Sonata in B flat major was conceived in tribute to him. Indeed, it has been seen as a kind of domesticated 'Hammerklavier', a sonata with which it shares its key, the contours of its opening motif and even (when it was published after Mendelssohn's death) its opus number (106). There, however, the resemblance ends. Mendelssohn's is a work of some charm, with a lyrical slow movement and a trademark scherzo tripping with mischievous sprites, but its want of depth is all the more conspicuous for the comparison it invites. Not so the fine keyboard piece he completed a few days afterwards, the Fugue in E minor, whose angular, anguished lines, climaxing in a benedictory chorale, betray their conception at the bedside of a dying friend. Mendelssohn later added a prelude and published the work in 1837 as the first of the Six Preludes and Fugues, Op. 35.

Number 3 Leipzigerstrasse was a house of strong opinions, and in following the current of his creative instincts during these months, Felix often found himself steering a choppy course between the Scylla and Charybdis of his parents' tastes. Just as Lea deprecated her son's excursions into what she saw as unperformably historicist sacred music, so Abraham deplored his fascination with Beethoven – the later the worse. Felix described his father as being 'in a constant state of irritation, incessantly abusing Beethoven and all visionaries' at this time, and such critical differences were clearly a source of genuine tension in the household. It is all the more indicative of Felix's growing independence of mind, therefore, that his next work represents his most profound engagement with Beethoven's rarefied late style.

CD 1 ④ Mendelssohn began work on his String Quartet No. 2 in A minor, Op. 13 in the summer of 1827. To the same summer belongs the song *Frage* ('Question'), a romantic lyric the words of which Felix may have written himself. The song has been linked with Felix's supposed feelings for Betty Pistor, a young member of the Singakademie choir whose attractions were surely not lessened by her father's ownership of Wilhelm Friedemann Bach's musical estate. Felix quoted the opening phrase of the song in the yearning *Adagio* and *Adagio non lento* sections which frame the quartet, beginning the first movement and ending the last. Whether or not the quartet thus has its roots in some amatory turmoil, it speaks a fractured, questing language

far removed from that of the Octet or *A Midsummer* *The Singakademie,*
Night's Dream, and clearly derives its formal impetus from *Berlin*
Beethoven's late quartets. The first and last movements
are similar in tone to those of Beethoven's own A minor
Quartet, Op. 132; the main theme of the slow movement
recalls the Cavatina from the B flat major Quartet, Op. 130;
and its fugal episode, which is further developed in the
finale, has something of the otherworldly spareness of the
fugal first movement of the Quartet in C sharp minor,
Op. 131. (The Fugue in E flat major for string quartet,
Op. 81 No. 4, composed six days after Felix completed the
A minor quartet, has similar resonances.) But there is more
than discipleship at work here, as witness the fact that the
'elfin' central section of the quartet's Intermezzo sounds
unexpectedly at home in its 'Beethovenian' surroundings.
Indeed, in confronting Beethoven's late quartets in his

own Op. 13, Mendelssohn, so often thought of as a musical conservative, arguably came closer than any of his contemporaries to assimilating to his own creative voice what was in the 1820s the cutting edge of the avant garde. He was never to rise in quite the same way again to the challenge of the contemporary. The String Quartet in A minor has no true successors in Mendelssohn's output, and remains in a sense his gateway to the road not taken.

Certainly the face the composer presented to the music-buying public in 1827 was a markedly less taxing one. The year saw his first published collection of solo songs, the Twelve Songs (*Zwölf Gesänge*), Op. 8, some of which dated from as long ago as early 1824. The set also includes three unattributed songs by Fanny. What to twenty-first-century sensibilities may seem an act of fraternal appropriation was, however, probably seen by Fanny herself as a way of smuggling her own compositions past the gender police: the songs did at least appear under their creator's surname, unlike, for example, the novels of the Brontës or George Eliot. Ironically, it was one of Fanny's contributions, *Italien*, which caught on, becoming one of the most popular of all Mendelssohn songs during the first half of the nineteenth century. Queen Victoria sang it as her party piece when Felix was a guest at Buckingham Palace in 1842, and afterwards, to his credit, he came clean about which of the Mendelssohns it really belonged to.

The String Quartet in A minor was completed on 26 October 1827, shortly after Felix's return from an extended walking holiday with friends, which had seen him tramping the Harz Mountains, Franconia, Bavaria and the Rhineland since the latter part of August. The trip seems to have helped restore his spirits after the *Camacho* debacle. On 31 August he wrote to Abraham by moonlight from Erbich ('a dump'):

If three of the most upstanding families in Berlin knew that three of their most upstanding sons were roving around the country roads at night with coachmen, peasants, and journeymen, and trading their life stories with them – they would be very disturbed – Don't be! For the sons are happy as larks.

A month later, with *Camacho* still very much on his mind, he seems to have walked himself into a state of buoyant defiance:

I have blazed a path for myself in instrumental music (and those are your own words, dear Father), but in other areas I have yet to. I know that I shall also be able to do so in the genre of opera, but I am also convinced that I have only just begun in the area of instrumental music; therefore I shall continue working until I find the opportunity to bring my ideas about opera to light, into the open, and you may believe my firm assurances that then I shall not be dissuaded, whether the work is well received or not.

The friends' wanderings took them to Frankfurt, where Felix attended a performance of Weber's *Oberon* and renewed his acquaintance with Ferdinand Hiller and the conductor Johann Nepomuk Schelble, both of whom he had met on his way to Switzerland five years earlier. In Baden-Baden he encountered the novelist and political writer Benjamin Constant, a friend of his aunt Jette, and in Heidelberg was deeply impressed by the jurist and champion of 'pure' music (namely sixteenth-century sacred polyphony) Justus Thibaut, from whose manuscript library he borrowed a setting by Antonio Lotti of the Matthean text *Tu es Petrus*. Mendelssohn would complete his own setting of the same words, the motet for five-part chorus and orchestra, Op. 111, in time to present it to Fanny on her birthday in November.

Back in Berlin Felix marked the family's third Christmas at Leipzigerstrasse with a 'Toy Symphony' ('Kindersymphonie'), now lost, for his younger sister Rebecka. He also produced a chorale cantata for chorus and orchestra, *Christe, du Lamm Gottes*, which braved Lea's displeasure by mining the same archaic seam that had produced the *Te Deum* and *Tu es Petrus*, and which would soon yield the chorale cantata *Jesu, meine Freude* for chorus and strings and the powerful *Hora est* for sixteen-voice choir and organ. (Disconcerted by Mendelssohn's choice of texts, other people had more spiritual concerns: there were mutterings among his friends that he might be turning Catholic.) With the recent departure of the family's lodger Karl Klingemann for a diplomatic posting in London, a cloud hung over the festivities for Fanny. (His absence, she wrote, left the household 'no longer so fairy-like: the true spirit of fun and pleasure is gone'.) But it had, as so often, a silver lining for her brother: Klingemann would prove tirelessly supportive in introducing Mendelssohn to the city with which he would soon establish one of his most fulfilling professional relationships.

The reception of *Camacho* may have buffeted Mendelssohn's curiously fragile self-confidence, but it seems not to have left a lasting dent on his reputation in Berlin's official circles. Indeed, at the beginning of 1828 his stock was visibly rising. The New Year saw the 300th anniversary of the death of the artist Albrecht Dürer, regarded by many as the fountainhead of German art, and Mendelssohn was commissioned by the Berlin Academy of Fine Arts to write a cantata as the centrepiece of the tercentenary celebrations in April. The text he had to work with was banal in the extreme, and the *Grosse Festmusik zum Dürerfest* for solo voices, chorus and orchestra is one of those occasional works that has signally failed to outlive its occasion. The work's unveiling was grandiose enough, though, with the Singakademie decked out in nationalistically Dürer-centric regalia, and Mendelssohn found himself the toast of the assembled dignitaries. At the dinner afterwards he was cheered to the rafters and awarded honorary membership of the Academy, Fanny noting how genuinely delighted he was by the tribute.

His second commission of the year was also a cantata, in this case to mark the opening in September of a huge international conference of scientists convened in Berlin by Alexander von Humboldt. Among the most remarkable figures of his, or indeed of any, age, Humboldt (quondam inspector of mines, explorer, mountaineer, philosopher, and a scientist to whom no branch of knowledge was alien or beneath study) was, by the time of his death in 1859, celebrated as one of the world's greatest intellectuals. Even his august patronage, however, has not saved Mendelssohn's 'Humboldt' Cantata from the obscurity into which it fell from the moment the final chord sounded.

Of far more significance than either of the commissioned cantatas is the work Mendelssohn composed between them. Like *A Midsummer Night's Dream*, the overture *Calm Sea and Prosperous Voyage* (*Meeresstille und glückliche Fahrt*), Op. 27, was inspired by a work of literature. In this case it was Goethe's pair of poems *Meeresstille* and *Glückliche Fahrt*, in which the poet recalls his experience of being dangerously becalmed off the coast of Capri in 1787 and the relief of feeling the wind rise again and the land heave into view. The poems had served, only six years earlier, as the inspiration for Beethoven's cantata of the same title. Whereas Beethoven had actually set Goethe's words, however, Mendelssohn creates instead a kind of musical correlative for the experience described in the poems (an experience, incidentally, that he had never known, having not yet travelled by sea). The overture is thus bipartite – 'two separate tableaux', as Fanny described it – with the first part representing the ominously still ocean, and the second, heralded by a tentative flute figure, the gathering motion of the vessel as the wind first ruffles then fills its sails. Goethe's poem ends with the line 'Schon seh' ich das Land!' ('Already I see the land!'), but Mendelssohn brings the boat safely into port in a coda replete with celebratory trumpet fanfares. At the very end the music subsides to calm again, but this time it is the calm of homecoming, untouched by the fears that underlay the opening tableau's evocation of Goethe's 'Tiefe Stille' ('Deep stillness'). Recognised by Mendelssohn's friend A.B. Marx as a milestone in the development of programme music, *Calm Sea and Prosperous Voyage* was first heard in a private performance on 7 September 1828, eleven days before the 'Humboldt' Cantata was premiered at the Singakademie. By that time, however, preparations were already well underway for a very different kind of first performance at the Singakademie, and one that would mark the climactic moment of the composer's gilded youth.

Mendelssohn's 1829 revival of Bach's *St Matthew Passion* has acquired almost mythical status in the history of music. Modern scholarship has nuanced the traditional account, but the occasion remains a seminal event both for Bach's music in particular and for the development of a musical canon in general. Certainly, Bach was by no means the forgotten figure of earlier versions of the myth. Mozart and Beethoven both knew his work well, and members of Mendelssohn's own family were important links in the chain by which Bach's music was preserved into the nineteenth century. Organists played his work throughout the German territories, and

Fanny Mendelssohn was far from alone among pianists in her devotion to *The Well-tempered Clavier*. While some of Bach's instrumental music thus remained familiar to the cognoscenti, however, his choral music had barely been heard in the eighty-odd years since his death. The scores of his motets, cantatas and Passions were hard to come by, and generally available only to scholars. Even so, a stirring of interest in this long-silent fund of music had been in the air for a few years. J.N. Schelble had put some of the smaller-scale works before the public in Frankfurt, as had Zelter from his locked cabinet at the Singakademie in Berlin. Zelter had even toyed with reviving the *St Matthew Passion* himself, but its awesome demands – not least in requiring a double choir and double orchestra – had blunted the edge of his good intentions. It took the youthful enthusiasm of his pupil and of Felix's friend Eduard Devrient to turn them into reality.

The two had been studying the *Passion* for some time. As we have seen, Mendelssohn had been given a copy of the score by his grandmother, and even before a public performance was mooted he had been directing friends in parts of the work at Leipzigerstrasse. What decided them to look for a more public stage remains unclear, though an announcement in Marx's music journal that Schlesinger, Mendelssohn's own first publisher, was planning to put the *Passion* into print may have played its part. Devrient, an actor from a theatrical family, gave a suitably dramatic account of events. According to him, he was so excited after singing in a complete run-through of the first part of the *Passion* at Mendelssohn's house one evening in January 1829 that he rushed round to Leipzigerstrasse first thing on the following morning, dragged Felix out of bed, convinced him that this music should be withheld from the public ear no longer, and badgered him into accompanying him to the

Singakademie. There the two young men bearded Zelter in his den and overcame all the old man's brusquely stated objections to a public performance ('Experienced people have given up the task and now two snotnoses behave as if the whole thing were child's play'). 'And to think,' Devrient has Felix exclaim at the end of their representations, 'that it has to be an actor and a young Jew who return to the people the greatest Christian music!' There was certainly a lot more to it than that – we know, for example, that the two friends had already booked the Singakademie hall in December and that Felix had agreed to arrange Handel's *Acis and Galatea* for Zelter in exchange for use of the choir. But whatever the actual course of events, on 2 February 1829 Felix began to direct choral rehearsals of the *Passion* at the Singakademie. It was the eve of his twentieth birthday.

The *St Matthew Passion* was performed on 11 March 1829 for the first time since Bach's death. It was a triumph. The Mendelssohns had been assiduous in inviting the great and the good, Marx had provided invaluable publicity, and tickets sold out within minutes. More than a thousand people had to be turned away. Felix, a figure of calm authority beyond his years, stood at a piano onstage, conducting with a baton (then still an unusual practice), and the music was heard, according to Fanny who sang among the altos, in a profound silence more typical of the church than of the concert hall. At the end, the enthusiasm of the audience and the press was unbounded. The influential critic Ludwig Rellstab spoke for all when he wrote of the 'eternally great, infinitely miraculous power and nobility of the work'. 'Almost never,' he continued, 'have we heard so perfect a performance... [Mendelssohn] accomplished the extraordinary through his devotion and unique talent.' A second performance was arranged, over Spontini's pusillanimous objections, for Bach's birthday on 21 March, and again the hall was packed. Goethe, reading Zelter's letters about the revival, replied from Weimar that he felt as if he heard 'the roar of the ocean from afar'.

The *St Matthew Passion*'s emergence under Mendelssohn's baton from its long years of silence served as the catalyst for a revival of Bach's music throughout the German lands and beyond. There would be setbacks along the way – not all the ensuing performances were as enthusiastically received, even by German audiences – but it is a revival which has continued to broaden and consolidate itself to this day. But 11 March 1829 can also be seen as the opening of a fault-line in Mendelssohn's own musical career. At the age of just twenty, he was now regarded not only as a composer and performer of genius but also as one of Europe's leading interpreters of the music of the past. The conflicting demands of these two roles would prove a source of increasing friction over the years that followed. For the moment, though, he was riding the crest of a wave. A third performance of the *Passion* took place at the Singakademie, with Zelter at the helm, on 17 April. But by then Mendelssohn – his fourth and final term at the University over – was already on his way to England for the first leg of a cultural grand tour that would see him travelling the length and breadth of Europe for the next three years.

Chapter 3

Grand Tourist
(1829–1832)

Grand Tourist (1829–1832)

Travel had been a part of Mendelssohn's education since childhood. The itinerary on which he embarked in April 1829 was also, in a sense, an educational one. Conceived as a necessary prelude to his professional career, it was at once an opportunity, as he himself put it, to 'consolidate [his] own taste', and an extended exercise in gathering information and contacts. As yet Mendelssohn was principally known to a musical public within the German territories – and even here, as *Camacho* had shown, there was no cast-iron guarantee of success. By getting to know other European centres of musical excellence, he would, so he and his father hoped, be able to make an informed decision as to where he might best put down his professional roots. (At a time when most musicians had to snatch at security wherever they found it, it is perhaps typical of the Mendelssohn family's outlook that they assumed their freedom of choice in the matter to be absolute.)

The tour fell into two parts. The first, lasting seven months, took him to London, Scotland and Wales. He then returned to Berlin for the winter and spring of 1829–30 before spending the next two years travelling through Germany, Austria, Italy, Switzerland and France, ending his itinerary in London, where it had begun. The wanderer sent home detailed impressions at every stage, and the tour is one of the most colourfully documented episodes of his life. It is also testimony to the rapid burgeoning of a young man's reputation and, in the best *Bildungsroman* tradition, to the development and impact of a remarkable personality.

Mendelssohn's first experience of a sea crossing reminded him of his *Calm Sea and Prosperous Voyage* in all the wrong ways. He took the steamer to England from Hamburg on 18 April and had the roughest of three-day passages. With engine breakdown adding to the natural obstacles of wind and fog, he was seasick to the point of fainting by the time they arrived in the Thames estuary. It was an inauspicious start to what turned out to be one of the most rewarding periods of his life.

He was greeted at the dockside by the familiar face of Karl Klingemann, one of several German expatriates who would help smooth his path into fashionable London society over the coming weeks. These included Ignaz Moscheles, who had arranged lodgings for him in the house of a well-to-do German metal merchant in Great Portland Street, and who, as one of the best-known figures on the London musical scene, also held the key to the doors of concert life in the capital.

Initially overwhelmed by the scale and busyness of the largest metropolis on earth, Mendelssohn was soon revelling in the breadth of opportunity it offered to a person of his talent and connections. Just around the corner from his lodgings were the twin centres of London concert-giving, the Hanover Square Rooms and the Argyll Rooms, the venues respectively of the Concert of Ancient Music and the Philharmonic Society. It was at the latter that Mendelssohn gave his first public concert in England, on 25 May. The work with which he introduced himself to the London musical public was his Symphony No. 1 in C minor, and it scored a great hit – 'greater', he wrote home, 'than I could ever have dreamed'. The novelty of his conducting with a baton was much noticed, and the central movements had to be encored. Five days later he gave a concert at which he performed Weber's *Konzertstück* from memory (also an unusual procedure at the time), and on 15 June he played his own *Variations concertantes* in D major, Op. 17 with the cellist Robert Lindley. This set of eight variations and coda on an original and not patently promising theme was written in January for his sixteen-year-old brother Paul, an able cellist. Nine days later Mendelssohn gave the English premieres both of his own overture to *A Midsummer Night's Dream* and of Beethoven's 'Emperor' Concerto (again from memory). The overture also featured in the programme of a massive fundraising event in July, which was energetically organised by Mendelssohn himself in aid of victims of flooding in Silesia. Among the other works in the concert was his Concerto in E major for two pianos, which he performed with Moscheles. From first to last, Mendelssohn was a sensation, his natural modesty, gentlemanliness and – perhaps most congenially to an English audience – determinedly amateur status eliciting as much comment as his breathtaking musical gifts. A portrait painted by James Warren Childe shows that he had also reinvented himself as an English dandy: one hand on hip, top hat in the other, he looks every inch the young man about town.

Mendelssohn's social life during these first months in London was if anything even more hectic than his musical one. He met, naturally, the leading lights of the music scene, including Sir George Smart (the director of the Philharmonic Society, who had been a guest of the Mendelssohns in Berlin), William Horsley (the glee composer with whose family Mendelssohn became close friends) and Thomas

Attwood (a living link to Mozart, whose pupil he had been in Vienna in the 1780s). Armed with letters of introduction, he also did the rounds of the nobility who were in town for the 'season', having a shouted conversation with the deaf Duke of Devonshire, and rubbing shoulders with the Duke of Wellington and other members of the establishment at fashionable balls. Aristocrats such as the Marquis of Lansdowne gave him tours of their private art collections, and the great engineer Isambard Kingdom Brunel showed him the unfinished Rotherhithe Tunnel under the Thames (a project of his father Sir Marc Isambard Brunel). He even had his cranial bumps felt at the offices of a fashionable phrenologist: 'music was supposedly the predominant characteristic', he noted, laconically.

Mendelssohn's drawing of Durham Cathedral, dated 24 July 1829

On 22 July Mendelssohn and Klingemann set off by coach from Charing Cross for a tour of Scotland. Travelling

via York and Durham, where Felix made a striking sketch of the cathedral in the album he kept with him throughout the journey, they arrived in Edinburgh four days later. Here the pair climbed Arthur's Seat, the volcanic outcrop above the city, and delighted in its panoramic views. 'Few memories of Switzerland could outdo this one,' Mendelssohn reported to his family. 'Everything looks so stern and robust here, even if it all is half obscured by steam or smoke or fog.' They attended a bagpipe competition in the company of the music journalist George Hogarth, and swam in the sea, which Mendelssohn found saltier than his last dip ('Doberan is lemonade by comparison'). He also visited Holyrood Palace. Here, at twilight in the ruined chapel where Mary Queen of Scots had been crowned, he 'found', he said, 'the beginning of my Scottish symphony'. (As the Mendelssohn scholar Peter Mercer-Taylor has pithily observed, it would be 1842 before he found the end.) For a cultural expeditionary with Mendelssohn's appetite, no trip to Scotland would have been complete without meeting the country's greatest literary lion, and the following day, 31 July, he and Klingemann visited Sir Walter Scott at his baronial residence, Abbotsford. The detour proved anticlimactic. Scott was about to leave home when they arrived and could spare them only half an hour's chit-chat, while they merely gawped in awe.

The next day the two friends set out for the Highlands, and by 3 August Felix was writing home from an inn at Blair Atholl in a storm so strong that it blew the internal doors open. From there the travellers made their way to Oban, where Mendelssohn sketched the ruins of Dunollie Castle, before boarding the steamer to Mull. Here, on 7 August, he began a letter to Abraham with a sketch of twenty-one bars of piano score with instrumental markings, 'in order to make clear what a strange mood has come over me in the Hebrides'. It was the opening of what would, three years and several incarnations later, become *The Hebrides* overture. Only the following day did he see Fingal's Cave, the extraordinary natural formation at Staffa off the west coast of Mull with which the overture has long been popularly associated. Klingemann memorably described the cave as looking 'like the inside of an immense organ, black and resounding, absolutely without purpose, and quite alone, the wide grey sea within and without'. Felix's own account of this emblematic voyage of early Romanticism is somewhat terser: 'horrible seasickness, Staffa'.

From the Hebrides the two young men made their way to Glasgow, and thence to Liverpool, where Klingemann took the coach for London, leaving his friend for the first time, as he melodramatically put it, 'completely alone, a stranger in foreign lands'. He was not so for long, decamping almost immediately to the Flintshire home of the Taylors, a mine-owning family with whom – especially the three daughters of the house – he had become friendly in London. The Three Fantasies or Caprices for piano, Op. 16 stand as a musical thank-you letter for the visit. Each supposedly represents an attribute of one of the daughters: the first, a bouquet of Anne's roses; the second some trumpet-like flowers in Honora's garden; the third, the rivulet by which he sketched with Susan. The composer called them his 'Welsh pieces' and regarded them, rose-tintedly, as among the best of his piano works. Abandoning plans for a short visit to Ireland because of the relentlessly rainy weather, which left 'the mountains looking like furniture, chandeliers, and rugs in some old palace, hidden beneath grey cloth covers, with only a few glorious corners poking out', he made instead a short tour of north Wales.

It was during this Welsh interlude that Felix wrote to Abraham wondering 'whether or not it was wholly right for me to be running around so haphazardly, without any real purpose, just for amusement' and answering himself in the affirmative because 'some new things were coming together in my head which proved to me that I... had to start composing again, which I had recently half doubted.' What with social calls, tourism, concert-going and concert-giving, his productivity had indeed taken a nosedive since he left Berlin in April. Back in London in the first week of September, however, Mendelssohn began to develop with Klingemann (wearing his librettist's hat) one of those pieces that had been coming together in his mind during their travels. This was a *Liederspiel* called *Heimkehr aus der Fremde* ('Homecoming from Abroad'), Op. 89 for his parents' silver wedding anniversary in December.

That occasion was in fact one of two forthcoming nuptial events in the Mendelssohn household. In January Fanny had finally become engaged to her suitor of many years, the artist Wilhelm Hensel, and their wedding was set for 3 October; Felix had been working in Wales on an organ piece for the occasion. On 10 September he wrote to Hensel with a mock-bureaucratic barrage of suggestions for the two festivities. Four days later he dated the autograph of his only major work of the summer, the String Quartet No. 1 in E flat major, Op. 12, often seen as a companion piece to the String Quartet No. 2 in A minor (the numbering reflects the order of publication). If the A minor quartet was inspired by Betty Pistor, the E flat quartet was covertly dedicated to her – covertly, that is, as far as Betty herself was concerned: it seems to have been an open secret in the Mendelssohn family. The hand of late Beethoven lies more lyrically on it than on its visceral predecessor, and there is less sense of straining against the boundaries of the form, even in the strenuous finale. The second movement, a wistful Canzonetta in Mendelssohn's characteristic 'elfin' mode, is sometimes played separately as a concert item.

No sooner had Mendelssohn completed the quartet than he was involved in a road accident that threw all his plans into disarray. His leg was trapped when a cab he was riding in overturned, and the injury laid him up for two months. To his immense chagrin, therefore, he missed his sister's wedding; even his organ processional failed to arrive on time, and Fanny spent her last night as a single woman composing a replacement. In the event, it was the end of November before he left England, working on *Heimkehr aus der Fremde* as he was jolted along snow-lined roads by post chaise, and it was 7 December before he saw Leipzigerstrasse again – for the first time in nearly eight months. Amazingly, the *Liederspiel* was completed just twelve days later. It was performed as planned on the evening of 26 December, before an audience of more than a hundred invited guests, on a double-bill with a hastily composed *Festspiel* by the newlywed Fanny Hensel, who had taken up residence with her husband in a wing of the Gartenhaus.

From the graceful opening bars to the cheerful communal conclusion, the overture and fourteen numbers of *Heimkehr* seem to epitomise the atmosphere of the Mendelssohn residence on high days and holidays. This is Mendelssohn operating happily in the comfort zone of family and friends, unconcerned about the public stage or the wider impact of his music. He even includes a part to be sung on a monotone by the tone-deaf Hensel (though Hensel still managed to get it wrong on the day!). There is something especially moving about the finale, which strikes a note of domestic *satisfaction* somehow more durable than mere celebration. It is a touching tribute to Felix's delight in his own homecoming and to the stability of a marriage that had lasted twenty-five years and provided him with one of the securest, if also one of the most demanding, childhoods of any major composer. Had anyone told him on that happy night that *Heimkehr* would be his last completed operatic work, Mendelssohn – who had received three offers from Covent Garden and Drury Lane in recent months – would probably have laughed them to scorn.

Mendelssohn remained with his family at Leipzigerstrasse until the beginning of May 1830. During this time he added the final numbers to his second set of Twelve Songs (*Zwölf Lieder*), published that year as Op. 9, which he had given Fanny musical power of attorney to start selecting while he was absent in the United Kingdom. (As in the Op. 8 set, three of the songs are by Fanny herself.) The first song in the set is the Betty Pistor-associated *Frage*, which had provided the framing sections for the A minor String Quartet. The beginning of 1830 also brought the offer of a newly created music professorship at the University of Berlin – a remarkable accolade for a twenty-one-year-old who had only finished his own studies there the year before. Mendelssohn, however, had the confidence to decline it, lobbying instead for his friend Marx, who was duly appointed. But above all, his sojourn in Berlin enabled him to complete a work that had been forming in his mind since at least the beginning of 1829, the 'Reformation' Symphony, Op. 107.

Like the *Grosse Festmusik zum Dürerfest*, Mendelssohn's second symphony was conceived for a tercentenary, in this case of the Augsburg Confession, the founding document of the Lutheran faith. Whether or not it was commissioned for Berlin's noisy celebrations of the anniversary on 25 June 1830 remains unclear, but it was certainly not performed at them, receiving its premiere only in 1832. The symphony travels in the same programmatic direction as *A Midsummer Night's Dream* and *Calm Sea and Prosperous Voyage*. Quasi-

Palestrinian polyphony and the 'Dresden Amen' (later used by Wagner as the Grail motif in *Parsifal*) are co-opted to represent Roman Catholicism in the first movement, while the monumental finale is built on the archetypal Lutheran chorale *Ein' feste Burg ist unser Gott* ('A mighty fortress is our God'), first announced by flutes alone. The second movement is a lively scherzo, the textures of which anticipate those of the 'Italian' Symphony, while the ensuing *Andante* is a brief interlude of reflection leading directly into the finale. While far from flawless – the last movement, in particular, struggles convincingly to integrate chorale and sonata elements – the 'Reformation' has retained a higher place in the symphonic repertoire than it did in the estimation of its composer. Mendelssohn withheld it from publication, and it was the last of the symphonies to appear in print after his death, hence the confusing designation No. 5.

The 'Reformation' Symphony was finished on 12 May 1830. The very next day, Felix set off on the second and longest part of his 'grand tour' – ultimate destination Italy – which would keep him from home for the next two years. Abraham accompanied him as far as Leipzig, father and son stopping en route in Dessau, where Moses Mendelssohn had been born just over a century earlier. Here, where his grandfather had been confined to the ghetto each night at curfew, Felix played Beethoven and Haydn trios with friends, and was entrusted by the Duchess with personal messages to be delivered in Italy. In Leipzig he courted the publishers Breitkopf & Härtel, who bought his A minor Quartet, and Hofmeister, who bought his E flat major Quartet and told him that a pirated copy of his Symphony No. 1 was already going the rounds of the city – a revelation no doubt galling and gratifying in equal measure. During a fortnight in Weimar he paid several visits to Goethe, with

[handwritten margin note: Friederike D. of Anhalt-Dessau (1796 – 1850)]

75

Goethe's inscription
to Mendelssohn on
a manuscript page
of Faust, May 1830

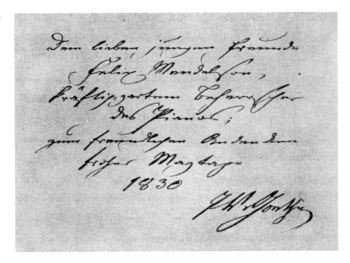

whom he engaged in long conversations about art and life. Nine years earlier Goethe's blessing had set the seal on Felix's reputation as a child prodigy. Now Mendelssohn sat day after day at the old man's piano, giving him a kind of one-to-one tutorial in the history of music by playing the works of key composers in chronological order from the sixteenth century to the present. Only with the modern did he meet a wall of incomprehension. 'That causes no emotion; it is only astonishing and grandiose,' was Goethe's verdict on one of the pieces: it was Beethoven's Fifth Symphony. When Mendelssohn left for Munich, Goethe gave him a manuscript page from *Faust* as a parting gift in memory of 'happy May days in 1830'. The two never met again.

In Munich, amid the usual social and musical whirl, Mendelssohn renewed his acquaintance with a prodigious seventeen-year-old pianist by the name of Delphine von Schauroth whom he had first met in Paris five years earlier. Felix's infatuation with her is as clear in his letters home to Rebecka as it was to the Bavarian royal circles in which he was moving: the following year the king himself asked Felix when he was going to make an honest woman of her. On 13 June he completed for Delphine the *Rondo capriccioso* in E major for piano, Op. 14 by adding 'sauce and mushrooms', as he self-deprecatingly put it, to an 1828 Étude in E minor.

In August he went on to Salzburg and Linz, where a comedy of errors (including his failure to recognise an elderly baroness as his mother's cousin) is retailed in a picaresque letter to Lea headed: '"How the travelling musician bore his great day of bad luck in Salzburg." Fragment of an unwritten diary by Count F. M. B.*** (Continued).' From Linz he took a piloted skiff down the Danube to Vienna, notating the sounds of church bells from the banks and lying on deck under the midnight stars 'as if I were eavesdropping on the music of the spheres'. The imperial capital itself failed miserably to match the city of his imagination, however. There were plenty of links to the glories of the recent musical past: he met many people who had known Beethoven, and the aged Abbé Stadler, a long-standing friend of Constanze Mozart, showed him the piano on which Haydn had composed *The Seasons*. But the glories themselves had left little trace in the salons and concert halls of a city already beginning to waltz to the strains of Strauss and Lanner. 'Beethoven is no longer here, nor Mozart or Haydn either', he wrote to Rebecka with a disappointment reminiscent of his vituperative letters from Paris in 1825. The composer and pianist Sigismond Thalberg is no more than 'a pretty hooked nose and stupendous fingers', while Carl Czerny is 'a tradesman on his day off, [who] says he is composing a lot now, for it brings in more than giving lessons'. In the face of an unsatisfactory present, Mendelssohn's cantata for solo voices, choir and orchestra on the chorale *O Haupt voll Blut und Wunden* ('O sacred head sore wounded'), written in Vienna in September, can perhaps be seen as a retreat into the certainties of a worthier age.

Italy seems to have held in the Mendelssohn family's collective imagination – and perhaps in Fanny's most of all – something of the place of Moscow for Chekhov's three sisters. It was thus with some excitement that Felix arrived in Venice in early October. There he worked on two of the sacred pieces that would go to make up his *Drei Kirchenmusiken*, Op. 23: 'Aus tiefer Noth schrei ich zu dir' and 'Ave Maria', the tender opening solo phrase of which he would remaster, many years later, in the striding coda to the 'Scottish' Symphony. He also reflected his impressions of the city in his first Venetian 'Gondellied' ('Gondolier's Song') for piano. Two years later this 'Venetianisches Gondellied', an hypnotic miniature in G minor, written for the absent Delphine, would appear in print as the final piece in his first collection of *Songs without Words* (*Lieder ohne Worte*), Op. 19b. From Venice he continued south to Florence where, when he was 'tired of all of the paintings, statues, vases, and museums' – and these were not joys of which he tired easily, as witness his reams of epistolary art criticism – he walked up into the surrounding hills and stumbled upon the tower supposedly used by Galileo for his experiments, now seemingly the focus of some Arcadian-sounding viticulture. Finally, on the evening of 30 October Mendelssohn left Florence for his true journey's end, Rome, where he was to spend most of the next eight months.

His letters from Rome are as vivid as ever in their observations on art, music, nature and the daily life of the city around him. He was much in demand, with a constant stream of invitations and callers to his flat in the Piazza di Spagna (near the Spanish Steps and the Casa Bartholdy, where his uncle Jacob had once held court). He loved the sunshine, and being surrounded by works of art. But there is also a new sense of self-containment as, in the absence of family or like-minded friends, he was thrown back more than ever before on his own resources. The musical life of the city came in for some familiar criticisms: 'The orchestras,' he reported, 'are beneath contempt, with neither pianists nor pianos... Even the papal singers are growing old, are almost completely unmusical, and don't even get the traditional pieces right.' The situation was made worse by the fact that Pope Pius VIII died less than a month after Mendelssohn's arrival, and large musical and social functions were suspended for the duration of the funeral and the ensuing long-drawn-out conclave to elect a new pontiff. Above all, Felix was saddened by what he saw as the Roman citizens' lack of respect for their own artistic heritage. The evidence of neglect he witnessed all around him – graffiti carved into monuments, cattle driven through the rooms of the Villa Madama – was, he wrote,

> *even worse than bad orchestras, and it must grieve painters even more than awful music does me. The people's spirits have probably been besieged and destroyed inside; they have a religion and they don't believe in it, they have a pope and a government but make fun of them, they have a splendidly bright past history but pay no attention to it. So it is no wonder that they take no pleasure in art, since they are indifferent even to all that is more serious.*

Even the priests at the pope's lying-in-state, he noticed, were whispering and laughing together.

Within three weeks of arriving in the Eternal City Mendelssohn completed the first version of a setting of Psalm 115 (*Non nobis Domine*) for solo voices, choir and orchestra, Op. 31, and the third of his *Drei Kirchenmusiken*: the austerely beautiful 'Mitten wir im Leben sind' for eight-voice choir. Other sacred works followed, including the benevolent

Verleih' uns Frieden for four-part choir, orchestra and organ; two of the motets for female chorus ('Veni Domine' and 'Surrexit pastor') that would appear as the Three Motets (*Drei Motetten*), Op. 39 in 1838; and the Lutheran chorale cantatas *Vom Himmel hoch* for solo voices, choir and orchestra and *Wir glauben all' an einen Gott* for choir and orchestra. It is almost as if he were continuing to wage against Rome's Catholic insouciance the campaign of high seriousness he had begun against the perceived frivolity of the Viennese. By the end of the year he had also finished what at this stage he called *Ouvertüre zur einsamen Insel* ('Overture to the Lonely Island') – the first version of *The Hebrides* overture, begun in such different climes sixteen months earlier.

One of the first people to hear, and be enchanted by, this early incarnation of *The Hebrides* was a volatile young Frenchman who arrived in Rome in March 1831. Hector Berlioz, then twenty-seven years old, had recently won, at his fourth attempt, the much sought-after Prix de Rome and had taken up his place at the city's French Academy. The first meeting of these two very different representatives of early Romanticism could easily have been their last. Berlioz recalled in his memoirs how the conversation had turned to his own prizewinning composition, *La Mort de Sardanapale* ('The Death of Sardanapalus'): 'On my revealing a positive dislike for the opening *allegro*, [Mendelssohn] exclaimed delightedly, "Thank heavens for that! I congratulate you... on your taste. I was afraid you might be pleased with it. Frankly, it's pretty awful."' Despite their radical divergence in temperament and musical personality, however, the two composers went on to spend much of the rest of the month in each other's company. They visited the tomb of Tasso together and they clambered among the ruins of the Baths of Caracalla, where Berlioz, ever the conversational *provocateur*, sought to shock Mendelssohn with his unorthodoxy in religious matters, only for Mendelssohn at that moment to lose his footing and fall down the remains of a steep staircase. 'Look at that for an example of divine justice,' Berlioz said, helping Mendelssohn to his feet. 'I blaspheme, you fall.' Mendelssohn's distaste for *Sardanapalus* extended to Berlioz's music in general – he would later say of the overture *Les Francs juges* that after reading the score he felt like washing his hands! – but, for all his impatience at the Frenchman's posturing, he clearly found him hard to resist as a companion. For his part, Berlioz held Mendelssohn in the highest respect as a composer, even if, as he famously observed after meeting him again twelve years later in Leipzig, he found him musically 'a little too fond of the dead'.

On 10 April, after sending Zelter detailed descriptions of the music of Holy Week, Mendelssohn left Rome with, among others, the artist Wilhelm von Schadow for a stay of almost two months in Naples. During that time he took in the ruins of Pompeii, the Sibyl's Cave at Cumae and the classical remains at Paestum, as well as a meeting with Donizetti, whom he represents as a sort of one-man opera factory. It seems to have been during the same visit that he finished planning the 'Italian' Symphony, though as with the 'Scottish' Symphony it would be a matter of years before it reached the form in which we know it today. Abandoning plans to continue to Sicily when Abraham stamped on the idea, Mendelssohn returned to Rome at the beginning of June. A few days later, on 18 June, he left the city for good, travelling north via Florence and Genoa to Milan. Here his musical encounters included Glinka, the so-called 'father of Russian music', and a fifty-six-year-old minor official of the Lombardy government by the name of Karl Thomas Mozart. One of the composer's two sons, Karl was a shy man, long resigned to the impossibility of escaping his father's shadow, and Mendelssohn must have felt the frisson of touching fingers across the generations as he played him another of the new compositions he had recently been sketching. This was the secular cantata *Die erste Walpurgisnacht* ('The First Walpurgis Night'), based on Goethe's 1799 dramatic ballad of the same name and in its final form one of Mendelssohn's most strikingly original works. From Milan, too, he wrote to Devrient, revealing that after the triumph of the *St Matthew Passion* revival he had been offered the directorship of the Singakademie in succession to Zelter. It would be a year before he arrived back in Berlin, but his thoughts were already turning to his future career.

Mendelssohn left Milan on 20 July and made his way through Switzerland, largely on foot and often in torrential rain, revisiting some of the sights of the family's trip in 1822, including daybreak from the summit of the Rigi. By mid-September he was in Munich, where he was reunited with Delphine von Schauroth. The deepening of their relationship is reflected in the scale of the music Mendelssohn wrote for her during this time. On 18 September he completed a two-movement showpiece for solo piano, similar in plan to the previous year's *Rondo capriccioso*. This time the sauce and mushrooms were added later, in the form of an orchestral accompaniment that transformed the work into the *Capriccio brillant*, Op. 22 in May 1832. In this guise it became one of Mendelssohn's regular concert standbys. Of far greater weight, however, is the Piano Concerto No. 1 in G minor, Op. 25 which Mendelssohn wrote at great speed after his arrival in the Bavarian capital. Dedicated to Delphine, it was premiered in the city on 17 October, with Mendelssohn himself at the keyboard, during a concert in the Odeon Hall at which he also directed the Symphony

No. 1 and *A Midsummer Night's Dream* overture. The first concerto Mendelssohn had written for seven years, it demonstrates a formal economy alien to his youthful works in the medium. It also reveals the powerful influence of Weber's *Konzertstück* on the mature composer. The three movements are connected both in their thematic content and by being played without a break. The piano and orchestra share the first-movement exposition, in which (given Mendelssohn's expressed aversion to the culture of virtuosity as exemplified by the likes of Frédéric Kalkbrenner and Franz Liszt) the soloist plays a surprisingly flamboyant role. Both the meditative slow movement and the extroverted finale are introduced by transitional brass fanfares, and towards the end of the finale Mendelssohn revisits the opening theme of the first movement.

Prominent among those seeking Mendelssohn's company in Munich was the Bavarian royal family itself. The composer gave a private performance at court, after which the queen remarked that she was so enraptured by his improvisation that 'one cannot think of anything else during the music' – a telling reflection on the usual royal listening habits. (Mendelssohn responded by apologising with ironic gallantry 'for carrying her away'.) It was during this visit that the king, whose conversation seems to have approached stream of consciousness, raised the question of marriage with Delphine. Mendelssohn, though clearly still smitten, appears discreetly to have distanced himself from the unfortunate girl thereafter, and two years later she married an English clergyman. Marriage was very much on the Mendelssohn family's minds back in Berlin, too, for on 5 November Felix's sister Rebecka, having rejected the advances of Eduard Gans, became engaged to the eminent mathematician Peter Lejeune Dirichlet, whom she married the following year.

Mendelssohn left Munich for Frankfurt with an opera commission in his pocket from the General Intendant of the Royal Theatre. While in Düsseldorf in late November he discussed possible subjects with the writer Karl Leberecht Immermann, who was soon to play an important part in his career. They seem to have plumped for *The Tempest* – Shakespeare had, after all, served the composer well in the past – but like so many opera projects over the years, this one was to join the ghostly ranks of Mendelssohn's theatrical might-have-beens. Meanwhile, in Frankfurt, he had renewed his friendship with Schelble, the director of the Cäcilienverein, who performed there some of the sacred works composed in Rome. Schelble's suggestion that Felix should write an oratorio fell on less stony ground than the projected Immermann collaboration. The seed was a long time germinating, but four years later it would flower in *St Paul*.

From Düsseldorf Mendelssohn continued to Paris, where he arrived on 9 December 1831. He found it in many respects a changed city from the one he had known in 1825. The July Revolution of 1830 had installed the 'citizen king' Louis Philippe on the throne and had brought to the streets and cultural life of the capital an atmosphere of political ferment alien to Mendelssohn's less radical sympathies. The musical scene, too, made a mixed impression on him. The musicianship of the Conservatoire orchestra was superlative, he told Zelter, but the 'fashionable music' of the capital was as indifferent as it had been in 1825. Among the old school of composers Cherubini still ruled the roost; while the rising star of the opera, Giacomo Meyerbeer, whose *Robert le Diable* was the talk of the town, so irritated Mendelssohn that he even had his hair cut short to avoid being mistaken for him. Felix did, however, make some new friends among the younger generation of composers and performers clustered in Paris around this time, including Chopin and Liszt. (The Hungarian rose dramatically in Mendelssohn's estimation after he faultlessly sight-read the G minor Piano Concerto.) Among his other new artistic friendships was one with the twelve-year-old piano prodigy Clara Wieck, who was later to escape the controlling grip of her father to become the wife of Robert Schumann.

During a stay of more than four months in the French capital Mendelssohn gave several concerts of his own and others' music, though his excited expectation that the 'Reformation' Symphony would receive its premiere there was cruelly disappointed after the Conservatoire orchestra found it 'too learned' at rehearsal – a reaction that seems permanently to have undermined Mendelssohn's own faith in the work. He also completed the Lutheran chorale cantata *Ach Gott, vom Himmel sieh' darein* (which the Mendelssohn scholar R. Larry Todd has seen as a sort of preliminary study for *St Paul*) and, more significantly for his future reputation, the secular cantata *Die erste Walpurgisnacht*.

Goethe's original ballad – not to be confused with the Walpurgisnacht episode in *Faust*, which had inspired the scherzo of the Octet – tells the story of heathen rites in the Harz mountains. The poet presents these goings-on as a response to the advance of Christianity: the heathens, determined to preserve the purity of their faith, scare away the Christian guards and watchmen by pretending to summon up the Christian devil. Why Mendelssohn, a devout Protestant, was attracted to such pagan fare must remain an open question, but in the overture and nine continuous numbers of *Die erste Walpurgisnacht* he created perhaps his most unconstrained masterpiece. Indeed, with the chorus of Druid guards and heathens (No. 6) the tone becomes positively orgiastic; one can see why Berlioz particularly admired the work. The cantata opens with a stormy orchestral evocation of winter and ends with a sublime choral paean to light which, but for its heathen text, would be quite at home as the culmination of a Christian sacred work (which is exactly what one listener misheard it as when the work was performed at a Sunday musicale in Leipzigerstrasse). *Die erste Walpurgisnacht* is audibly the creation of an opera composer *manqué*, and provides a tantalising glimpse of what Mendelssohn might have achieved on the operatic stage had he been able to find in his maturity a libretto that inspired him as Goethe did. The cantata was premiered at the Singakademie on 10 January 1833, but Mendelssohn was unsatisfied with it, returning to the score a decade later to produce the version finally published as his Op. 60.

While he was in Paris Mendelssohn learnt of two deaths that shook him profoundly. The first was that of his old friend the violinist Eduard Rietz, in whose memory he immediately composed the new Intermezzo for his String Quintet, Op. 18. The second was that of Goethe himself. Within days death drew even closer to hand when Paris was engulfed by an epidemic of cholera, which had already claimed the life of Mendelssohn's Aunt Jette in Berlin the previous year. Mendelssohn himself developed symptoms, albeit in a mild form, which delayed his departure from France. By 22 April, however, he was back in London, where his grand tour had begun three years earlier.

London too was a city in the grip of political change, with tensions running high in the lead-up to the passage of the great electoral Reform Act (Mendelssohn attended at least one meeting on the subject). In other respects, though, his arrival was a kind of homecoming: he even stayed in the same lodgings in Great Portland Street that he had occupied in 1829. Once again he was among trusted friends and familiar faces: Klingemann met him off the boat; Moscheles partnered him in private and public concerts, including a performance of Mozart's Concerto for two pianos, K. 365, for which Mendelssohn wrote special cadenzas; and the orientalist Friedrich Rosen, whom he had known in Berlin and who had become a close friend during his previous London stay, was a regular breakfast visitor. Attwood invited Mendelssohn to play the organ in St Paul's Cathedral, and his house in Norwood provided refuge from a pace so frenetic that Klingemann felt he needed a year to recover from just watching his friend's activities. Nor had the wider English public forgotten him. Writing to his father, Mendelssohn recalled that on 5 May he attended a Philharmonic rehearsal and was making his way down to the lobby when

> *someone called out from the orchestra:* There is Mendelssohn, *whereupon they all began yelling and clapping such that for a while I didn't know what to do, and when it was over, another called out* Welcome to him, *whereupon they struck up the same racket and I had to make my way through the hall and to the orchestra in order to make a bow. You see, I shall not forget that, for it was more dear to me than any other distinctions; it showed that the musicians are fond of me and were glad that I had come, and it was a happier moment for me than I can say.*

He gave performances of works written since his last visit, including the G minor Piano Concerto ('the triumph was ridiculous,' Klingemann reported) and the premieres of the *Capriccio brillant* and, under the confusing title *The Isles of Fingal*, the newly revised *Hebrides* overture.

CD 1 ⑦

Also sometimes known as 'Fingal's Cave', *The Hebrides* (*Die Hebriden*), Op. 26 represents a new strand in Mendelssohn's exploration of the possibilities of 'descriptive music'. Whereas *A Midsummer Night's Dream* and *Calm Sea and Prosperous Voyage* are musical reactions to works of literature, *The Hebrides* is first and foremost an evocation of the spirit of place. As we have seen, the beginning came to the composer spontaneously in Scotland. But he worked long and hard to keep the music true to that original inspiration. From Paris, for example, he had written to Fanny complaining that 'the entire, so-called working-out tastes more of counterpoint than of train oil, gulls, and salted cod – it should be just the other way around'. Forged over many months and in many different places, the resulting music nonetheless seems as natural an outgrowth of the landscape and seascape of the Western Isles as the mysterious hushed expansiveness of those opening bars. Today it is one of the best loved of all Mendelssohn's compositions, but after its first airing it received a mixed reception: one London critic saw in its composer 'one of the finest and most original geniuses of the age', while for others the overture's almost impressionistic tone-painting elicited only incomprehension.

It was in London, too, that Mendelssohn completed his first set of *Songs without Words* (*Lieder ohne Worte*), published later in the year in French, German and English editions, and known today as Op. 19b. These six short piano pieces stand at the head of a succession of eight collections of *Songs without Words* (two of them posthumous) which have perhaps done more than any other category of music to define Mendelssohn's image, for better or worse, in the popular imagination. After a slow start, the 'songs' attained the impetus of a musical phenomenon, identifying Mendelssohn for generations of music lovers with a (largely

website ⟩

feminine) tradition of amateur drawing-room pianism and a strain of easy lyricism bordering on the sentimental. The most famous items, such as the 'Spring Song', Op. 62 No. 6, are by now so familiar as to have become irredeemably hackneyed, but in origin the *Songs without Words* represent a new and distinctive musical genre, neatly defined by R. Larry Todd as 'textless piano miniatures that imitate features of art song'. The designation 'songs without words' seems to have been Mendelssohn's own and may have had its origins in a game that Felix and Fanny used to play as children, in which they made up words to fit the music of instrumental pieces. Over the years the 'songs' attracted several more or less fanciful titles and much speculation as to their extra-musical meaning, a subject on which Mendelssohn himself always refused to be drawn. Indeed, it was in response to one such enquiry that he issued what is perhaps his most famous, if highly contentious, statement on the power of music and its relation to the power of words. 'So much is spoken about music and so little is said,' he wrote to a former student in 1842:

> For my part I do not believe that words suffice for such a task, and if they did I would no longer make any music. People usually complain that music is too many-sided in its meanings; what they should think when they hear it is so ambiguous, whereas everyone understands words. For me, it is precisely the opposite, not only with entire speeches, but also with individual words. They too seem so ambiguous, so vague, so subject to misunderstanding when compared with true music, which fills the soul with a thousand better things than words. The thoughts that are expressed to me by the music I love are not too indefinite to put into words, but on the contrary, too definite. And I find every effort to express

such thoughts legitimate, but altogether inadequate... Only melody can say the same thing, can arouse the same feelings in one person as in another, a feeling that cannot be expressed by the same words.

When Goethe died in March, Mendelssohn had predicted that Zelter would not long survive him. In London Felix received the news that his old teacher had indeed died, on 15 May 1832. Zelter's death closed a chapter in Mendelssohn's own life, but it also marked a period in the life of his home city. Zelter had been the director of the Berlin Singakademie for almost as long as anyone could remember, and his demise left vacant the post Mendelssohn had apparently been offered after the triumph of the *St Matthew Passion* three years earlier. With his departure from London now imminent, events seemed to be conspiring, in unwelcome concentration, to force a decision on his next move.

As Mendelssohn's long journey drew towards its end he had been giving ever more consideration to its implications for his future. From Frankfurt in November 1831 he had written a long and thoughtful letter to Abraham, proudly enclosing the letter of commission for the Munich opera and opening the whole subject of his professional life in 'the time after my return'. In Dessau Abraham had apparently informed Felix that his grandmother Bella Salomon had left him a substantial legacy. 'Do you wish me to avail myself of this money...' Felix asks, 'or should I start all by myself and without any auxiliary money except what I have earned?' His own stated preference is to use the money, so as not to have to grub around for income from teaching or recitals ('which would hardly advance me'). He seeks Abraham's views on whether he should look for a post at a theatre. For his part, though, he feels too young and lacking in authority to be tied down to a music directorship that would entail 'such a mass of small details, dissipations, intrigues, etc.'. 'It could well happen,' he continues, 'that I might become involved in matters which would distract me – at least temporarily – from my main object (composition)' – a fear that would prove all too prescient. Whatever his reservation about music directorships, however, his grand tour had taught him one incontrovertible lesson. As he had written to Zelter from Paris,

> after all the beauties I had savoured in Italy and Switzerland, after all of the wonderful things that I experienced – and in particular while en route through Stuttgart, Heidelberg, Frankfurt, and down the Rhine to Düsseldorf: That was really the high point of my trip – for there I noticed that I was a German and wanted to live in Germany, as long as I could do so... and so I hope that in Berlin I shall be able to find my own livelihood...

Or, as he put it in the letter to his father, written during precisely those days in which he rediscovered his sense of oneness with his homeland: 'Never did I feel so clearly that I am a German in my heart and must always remain one...'

As far as the Singakademie directorship was concerned, though, he found himself in an awkward position. Having accepted an informal offer of the post in 1829, he believed that he was honour-bound to take it up, however reluctantly, if the offer still stood. But things had gone very quiet in the interim, and he was in no mood to stir them up. In particular, his London experiences had taught him that there might be a ready market for his talents as a composer, and he was deeply averse to the idea of putting himself forward for the Singakademie job if it was opened to general application.

The dilemma was still unresolved when Mendelssohn boarded the boat for the Continent at the end of June 1832. His return crossing of the Channel was as stormy as the outgoing one at the start of his great journey three years earlier. This time, however, the waters ahead would be just as turbulent.

Chapter 4

Düsseldorf
and Leipzig
(1832–1836)

"It would be a matter of difficulty to decide in which quality Mendelssohn excelled the most – whether as composer, pianist, organist, or conductor of an orchestra..."

Düsseldorf and Leipzig (1832–1836)

On 25 June 1832 Mendelssohn crossed the threshold of No. 3 Leipzigerstrasse for the first time in nearly two years. Delighted though he was to see his family again, the joy of homecoming soon evaporated in claustrophobia. After the heady freedom of his travels, Berlin seemed more provincial and conservative than ever, in both its musical and its political life. Even the weather was oppressive, and he found himself suffering from headaches and lethargy. In September he wrote to Klingemann that he was 'unspeakably depressed', and he would soon describe the restless and largely unproductive weeks after his return as 'the most bitter moments I ever endured, or ever could have imagined'. Above all, the question of the Singakademie directorship weighed heavily on him. He would have been happy enough for the post to pass uncontested to the acting director, Carl Friedrich Rungenhagen, who had been Zelter's deputy at the Singakademie for almost two decades; but under family pressure, and after Devrient's attempts to broker a joint directorship with Rungenhagen had collapsed, he eventually allowed his name to go forward as an alternative candidate. It was a disastrous decision. In the election on 22 January 1833 Rungenhagen swept the board with 148 votes to Mendelssohn's 88. For Abraham, the rejection was an affront to the family, who resigned *en masse* from the institution they had supported for so many years. For the hypersensitive Felix, it was a very public defeat in a battle he had not wanted to join, for a crown he had no desire to wear. Offered the deputy directorship as a consolation prize, he replied 'with polite expressions, that they could go hang themselves'.

Bitter though the blow undoubtedly was, however, there were more solid consolations to be had. For one thing, Prussian audiences proved highly receptive to the music he had been composing since he last appeared before them. Berlin performances of such works as *Die erste Walpurgisnacht, The Hebrides*, the 'Reformation' Symphony and the First Piano Concerto were themselves a shot in the arm for the city's concert life and garnered ecstatic reviews. More encouraging still was the continuing interest of his friends abroad. In November the Philharmonic Society approached him with a lucrative commission for three London works: a symphony, an overture and a vocal piece. For the second of these, Mendelssohn would in the event fob them off with the recycled 'Trumpet' Overture of 1826, while the vocal commission was fulfilled in April 1834 by the concert aria *Infelice* for soprano and orchestra, Op. 94. Far the most important effect of the commission, however, was the stimulus it gave to the completion of the 'Italian' Symphony, which Felix had committed to paper by 13 March 1833.

Work on the Symphony took up most of Mendelssohn's creative energies during the early part of 1833, but he also produced a succession of smaller compositions during these weeks, including a couple of pieces for the unusual combination of clarinet and basset-horn, Opp. 113 and 114; the three-movement Fantasia in F sharp minor for piano, Op. 28, also known as the *Sonate écossaise*; and in February the *Responsorium et Hymnus* for male voices, cello, bass and organ, Op. 121. In the same month K.L. Immermann, whose projected operatic collaboration with Mendelssohn had collapsed when the composer rejected his libretto, asked Felix instead to write the incidental music for a play he was mounting as the new director of Düsseldorf's theatre: Calderón's *Der standhafte Prinz* ('The Constant Prince'). The commission, small beer in itself, opened the door to a much more significant approach from Düsseldorf in March, when Felix was offered the directorship of the Lower Rhine Music Festival – the fifteenth in a prestigious annual series of festivals, scheduled to be held in the town at the end of May. Chafing under his confinement to Berlin, Mendelssohn did not need asking twice. Even though he was already committed to premiering the 'Italian' Symphony in London earlier the same month, he immediately accepted the offer. He stopped off in Düsseldorf to discuss the festival programme on his way to England in April, and amazed Immermann by playing Beethoven's 'Pastoral' Symphony from memory on the piano and conducting a rehearsal of the work without a score.

On 25 April he arrived in London for his third visit to the city he called 'the dear, old, smoky nest', and reinstalled himself in his familiar Great Portland Street lodgings. With Moscheles he performed a jointly composed set of bravura variations on the gypsy march from Weber's incidental music to P.A. Wolff's *Preciosa*, the *Variations brillantes*. He also accompanied the Mephistophelian violin virtuoso Paganini (whom Fanny had once described as looking like a cross between a monkey and a deranged murderer), and on 13 May conducted the premiere of his 'Italian' Symphony at a Philharmonic concert in which he also played Mozart's great D minor Piano Concerto, K. 466 from memory. The new symphony was a resounding success with audience and critics alike, *The Harmonicon* confidently declaring it a work that 'will endure for ages'. It has. One of the finest of all Mendelssohn's compositions, the symphony has an irresistible *brio* that belies its protracted birth. Indeed, there can be few more gladdening evocations of Keats's 'warm south' than the effervescent opening movement. The ensuing *Andante* has the mysterious gravity of a religious procession, while the third movement, a graceful *Menuetto*, transports us to the elegant ballrooms of the Italian nobility. By contrast, the open-air finale erupts in a motoric folkdance, the *saltarello*, bringing a raw sunburnt edge to the Symphony's irrepressible energy. Amid the plaudits of the London audience, only the composer himself seemed dissatisfied and, as with so many of his compositions, he immediately began to revise the score. No amount of tinkering could convince him that it was fit for publication, however, and it appeared in print only after his death, as the Symphony No. 4 in A major, Op. 90.

Five days after the premiere Felix left England for Düsseldorf. Arriving there on 20 May, he unpacked his bags as the house guest of his old Roman acquaintance, the painter Wilhelm von Schadow, who was director of the city's Academy of Arts. He launched straight into rehearsals for the two festival concerts, which took place on 26 and 27 May. The first featured – in addition to the ever reliable 'Trumpet' Overture – Handel's oratorio *Israel in Egypt*, the manuscript of which Mendelssohn had ferreted out at the Royal Music Library during his London stay. The second included Beethoven's 'Pastoral' Symphony and third *Leonore* overture. Abraham came to Düsseldorf for the occasion, which provided him with his first real exposure to the rounded public professional his son had become. As he reported to Lea, it was an eye-opener for him:

I have never seen anyone so petted and courted as Felix is here. He himself cannot sufficiently praise the zeal of all the performers in the festival, and their confidence in him; and, as everywhere, he astonishes and moves everyone with his playing and his memory.

A few days later, on Whit Sunday, Abraham again wrote in wonder to his wife:

To me at least, it does appear like a miracle that four hundred persons of all sexes, classes and ages, blown together like snow before the wind, should let themselves be conducted and governed like children by one of the youngest of them all, too young almost to be a friend for any of them, and with no title or dignity whatever.

The concerts were so enthusiastically received by the thousand or so who attended them that, unprecedentedly for the festival, an extra one was mounted on 28 May, at which Felix, in addition to encoring items from the earlier concerts and airing some new ones, also appeared at the keyboard in Weber's *Konzertstück*. Beethoven's old friend Anton Schindler, later a persistent critic of Mendelssohn's conducting, found in the performers 'a zeal such as I have never before witnessed' and had no doubt where its origins lay:

The exactness and indefatigable industry of the General Director, the excellent Felix Mendelssohn-Bartholdy, are responsible for the quality of the performance. It is due to him alone that the fifteenth Lower Rhine Festival was incomparably superior to all preceding ones.

Title and dignity would not be long in following. By the end of the proceedings Abraham was able to report that Felix had been offered, and had accepted, a three-year post as music director to the municipality of Düsseldorf, beginning in October – a central plank of Immermann's ambitious project to re-energise the town's cultural life. Under the terms of his agreement, Mendelssohn would be responsible for church music and a maximum of eight concerts a year; he would also, on slightly hazy terms, direct the city's opera. The job was well paid, and came with three months' holiday a year. Forgotten, it seems, were the potential distractions that had put him off a music directorship when he canvassed the subject with Abraham two years earlier. Now, in the first flush of freedom from the narrowing prospect of Berlin, he could, as he wrote to Julius Schubring, see the possibility of 'quiet and leisure for composition' in his new post.

It was thus in thoroughly restored spirits that Mendelssohn travelled from Düsseldorf to London at the beginning of June 1833, on his fourth visit to England. Abraham came along for the ride, his letters home providing wry and occasionally scandalised commentary on the country's manners, sights and weather. Five days after their arrival they attended the Philharmonic concert at which the multipurpose 'Trumpet' Overture was given yet another outing, this time in apparent fulfilment of the second part of the Society's commission. Five days later still, on 15 June, Mendelssohn stood godfather at the christening of Ignaz and Charlotte Moscheles's son, Felix, for whom he wrote a lullaby later published as the sixth of his Six Songs (*Sechs Lieder*), Op. 47. Together, Felix and Abraham hit the tourist trail, visiting the Royal Observatory at Greenwich and the naval dockyards at Portsmouth, and briefly crossing the Solent to the Isle of Wight. By then, however, Abraham was

suffering from a weirdly similar injury to the one that had
delayed Felix in London at the end of 1829. He had gashed
his leg while looking over a man-of-war in Portsmouth,
and much of the rest of Mendelssohn's time in London
was spent tending to the invalid. His duties as nurse did
not, however, prevent his flirting with Mary Alexander, the
daughter of a Scottish laird, who developed a serious crush
on him. Nor did they keep him from attending Parliament
to observe, with disturbingly breezy detachment, the passage
of the Jewish Civil Disabilities Act, which Abraham saw
as the greatest emancipatory measure in the entire post-
Christian history of Judaism. By 25 August the older man
was sufficiently recovered for them to set off home, only for
the curse of the Mendelssohn leg to strike yet again: while
visiting his brother Joseph in Horchheim Abraham stepped
on a nail and had to take to his bed once more. As a result, it
was 13 September before father and son reached Berlin. The
latter's arrival came as a pleasant surprise, since Abraham (in
one of those mischievous charades which the Mendelssohns
seemed to relish, but which lose so much in translation from
the family circle) had told Lea he was travelling not with
Felix but with a painter called Alphonse Lovie!

After just three days at Leipzigerstrasse Mendelssohn
was on the road once more, travelling to Leipzig en route
to Düsseldorf, where he arrived in October to take up his
music directorship. He threw himself into the role with his
customary purposefulness: drilling the often ill-disciplined
musicians in the works of Beethoven, Mozart, Haydn and
Handel; trawling the libraries of neighbouring cities for
suitable sacred music, including masses and motets by
such then little-known composers as Palestrina and Lassus;
mounting concerts both for civic occasions and for visiting
dignitaries (including in October 1833 the crown prince

of Prussia, who, as Frederick William IV, was later to play a key part in Mendelssohn's professional fortunes). From the first, though, it was clear that the post would be all too subject to the 'mass of small details, dissipations, intrigues, etc.' that he had feared as the inescapable lot of the music director. Indeed, his first-ever public opera performance, a staging of Mozart's *Don Giovanni* in December, was almost sunk by them. Tensions were already evident during the twenty rehearsals, and on the first night the curtain had to be lowered repeatedly when audience protests at high ticket prices erupted into catcalls during the music. It was only by a supreme effort of self-control that Mendelssohn stopped himself from throwing down his baton and stalking offstage, and he refused to direct a second performance until he had received a formal apology from the troublemakers – a strategy that seems to have gained him the lasting respect of his musicians. It was an ominous start to his tenure, though, especially since Immermann, as a playwright, set greater store by the public stage than by any other aspect of his self-imposed mission of regeneration.

Düsseldorf was a picturesque town surrounded by vineyards, and Mendelssohn had good friends there, including the von Schadows with whom he was lodging. He also led an active social and recreational life that even extended to a newfound passion for horse riding. Despite the superficial attractiveness of this new environment, however, Mendelssohn found that as the months went by the frustrations of his job increased significantly. Not the least of these was the lack of precisely that 'quiet and leisure for composition' he had naively expected it to provide. He was, after all, a very public figure in the town, and if his duties did not interrupt his writing, visitors often did. As a result, while he continued to revise existing works – a habit that would become a compulsion over the years – the Düsseldorf period was a conspicuously thin time for new compositions. Prime amongst them is the overture *The Fair Melusine* (*Die schöne Melusine*), which he wrote in November 1833, apparently for the Philharmonic Society in London, where Moscheles premiered it on 7 April the following year. The overture seems to have originated in Mendelssohn's dissatisfaction with Conradin Kreutzer's opera on the well-known legend of an undine, or water spirit, who takes on human form when she falls in love with a mortal knight. His own treatment of the story, whose protagonists appear to be represented by the contrasting principal themes, begins and ends with a gently rippling melody that found an echo twenty years later in the opening music of Wagner's *Das Rheingold*.

In January 1834, a couple of months after finishing the overture, he completed the *Rondo brillant* for piano and orchestra, Op. 29, a lively but somewhat routine showcase for his pianistic talents. 'My own poverty in shaping new forms for the pianoforte once more struck me most forcibly whilst writing the Rondo,' he admitted to Moscheles, its dedicatee. 'It is there I get into difficulties and have to toil and labour, and I am afraid you will notice that such was the case.' Meanwhile, he struggled to find time for his projected magnum opus, the oratorio *St Paul*, which was scheduled for performance at the Frankfurt Cäcilienverein in December 1835. He had been crafting the libretto for many months – with Schubring providing theological consultancy by post – but composition had to be fitted around his executive commitments in Düsseldorf, and not until April 1834 did he begin serious work on the music. By then those commitments had grown to embrace the musical supervision of Immermann's pet project, a new municipal theatre due to open later in the year.

This addition to Mendelssohn's workload proved the straw that broke the camel's back. Temperamentally unsuited to the nitty-gritty of theatre administration – which included responsibility for the auditioning of singers, the commissioning of sets and even the state of the actors' costumes – he conscripted the cellist Julius Rietz, the brother of his late friend Eduard, to deal with the day-to-day management as second conductor. But there was plenty to do to get things up and running even after Rietz assumed the post in September, and Mendelssohn had neither patience nor aptitude for the personnel aspects of the task. As he later wrote to Devrient:

> To wrangle with a creature for two *Thaler*; to be severe with the good, and lenient with the good-for-nothing; to look grand in order to keep up a dignity that no one believes in; to seem angry without anger; all these are things which I cannot do, and would not if I could.

It was an impatience that spilled over into other areas of his music directorship, too. In October, for example, he threatened to resign as director of church music unless an incompetent organist was replaced – an over-reaction symptomatic of the stress under which he was now operating. To make matters worse, Mendelssohn's relationship with Immermann – the tie that bound together their disparate investments in the town – was rapidly unravelling into suspicion and recrimination. It finally broke on 10 November 1834 when, three days after directing a performance of Weber's *Oberon*, Mendelssohn, furious at his colleague's perceived lack of support, peremptorily resigned as intendant of the Düsseldorf opera. Immermann's new theatre had been open for just two weeks.

Abraham Mendelssohn was outraged at what he saw as an act of petulant irresponsibility. He accused his son of 'gruffness and violence, of grabbing things quickly and dropping them just as quickly'. Not only had Felix fallen at the first hurdle of a career so long and meticulously planned; he had also shown himself unworthy of his employers' trust: 'Through your own calamitous stubbornness you have done yourself more harm than you yet know', Abraham wrote. 'But – and this is more important – you could have brought misfortune on a whole institution which you yourself encouraged and now have thoughtlessly deserted.' Abraham was not alone in his disapproval. Even Devrient deplored his friend's 'snappish temper', while Immermann described Mendelssohn as 'totally wild' when he tried to patch things up with him a few weeks later.

The composer himself seemed remarkably untroubled by all this opprobrium. For one thing, shedding his operatic responsibilities enabled him to concentrate on *St Paul*. For another, he was already receiving alternative offers. On a visit to Leipzig at the end of September 1834 he had been sounded out about the possibility of working there, and in January 1835 he was offered a professorship at the university, which he declined with an appealing mixture of false modesty and clear-headed self-awareness:

I am in no way in a position to speak on music properly for even a half hour, let alone throughout an entire colloquium, and I don't think I could learn to do so even if my entire well-being depended on it. Not once have I ever been able to follow an entire colloquium satisfactorily, and always came away feeling more unmusical than I did when I went in, so that little by little I set myself the goal of being a practical musician and not a theoretical one.

After his recent experiences, he also found it easy to turn down an offer to direct the opera in Munich. In mid-January, however, he was approached again by the Leipzig authorities, this time to be offered the directorship of the city's Gewandhaus concerts. One of the most prestigious openings in the German musical world, the position also came with the promise of six months' holiday a year (the Gewandhaus season ran from the beginning of October to the beginning of April). This was twice Mendelssohn's Düsseldorf entitlement and, for a man whose primary focus remained composition, was in itself a powerful incentive to acceptance. Negotiations continued through the early months of the year; perhaps chastened by his father's criticisms of irresponsibility, Mendelssohn consulted Abraham in detail about the offer and was at particular pains to establish that no internal candidate would be displaced by his taking it up. By the end of April, however, everything had been hammered out, and on 1 May he formally resigned his music directorship in Düsseldorf, having served only half his contractual period.

The very same day, his second collection of *Songs without Words*, Op. 30 appeared simultaneously across Europe in German, French and English editions. Unlikely as it may seem, given the genre's later popularity, this was a risky venture for the publishers. Mendelssohn's previous Op. 19b collection had sold only a handful of copies in England. Nonetheless Mendelssohn followed the pattern of the first book very closely, compiling a set of six contrasting pieces, beginning with a lyrical 'solo' song and ending with another melancholy Venetian 'Gondellied', this time in F sharp minor. The second piece, an *Allegro di molto* in B flat minor, was originally written to mark Sebastian Hensel's birth in June 1830, its agitation reflecting something of his nephew's difficult passage into the world. The whole opus was dedicated to Elise von Woringen, the daughter of Otto von Woringen, a senior Düsseldorf judge who was one of Felix's closest friends in the town he was about to leave.

On 13 June Mendelssohn signed on the dotted line with the Leipzig authorities. A few days earlier he had conducted his second Lower Rhine Music Festival – the seventeenth, this time held in Cologne – with Fanny singing in the chorus, and Hensel, Abraham, Lea and Rebecka among the audience. It was another triumphant success, and one of those present – the English composer Julius Benedict – left an awed account of Mendelssohn's command from the platform:

> It would be a matter of difficulty to decide in which quality Mendelssohn excelled the most – whether as composer, pianist, organist, or conductor of an orchestra: nobody certainly ever knew better how to communicate, as if by an electric fluid, his own conception of a work to a large body of performers. It was highly interesting, on this occasion, to contemplate the anxious attention manifested by a body of more than five hundred singers and performers, watching every glance of Mendelssohn's eye, and following, like obedient spirits, the magic wand of this musical Prospero... Need I add, that he was able to detect at once, even among a phalanx of performers, the slightest error either of note or accent?

Mendelssohn fulfilled the last of his Düsseldorf contractual obligations on 2 July, conducting a concert that included Beethoven's Seventh Symphony and his own *Calm Sea and Prosperous Voyage*. By the end of the month he was back in Berlin for a five-week stay with his family in preparation for the challenges ahead.

So it was that on 30 August 1835 Mendelssohn arrived in the town that was to be his principal home for the remaining twelve years of his life. Leipzig was a wealthy city of some 45,000 people, more than twice the population of Düsseldorf. Famous for its trade fairs, it was also an intellectual centre of excellence, with an ancient university and a thriving

The young music director: Mendelssohn in 1835, by Wilhelm von Schadow

107

publishing scene, to which the twenty-five-year-old Robert Schumann had recently contributed a campaigning voice with the launch of his music journal, the *Neue Zeitschrift für Musik*. Johann Sebastian Bach had spent the last quarter-century of his life there as Cantor of St Thomas's – an association of particular satisfaction to the incoming Berliner – and the city's musical traditions remained second to none in the German territories.

The Gewandhaus Orchestra had a justified reputation as perhaps the finest of all German ensembles. Forty-strong and established for more than half a century by the time Mendelssohn took the helm, it derived its name from the city's Clothiers' Hall, within which was the specially constructed auditorium where it gave its annual series of concerts. The venue could accommodate 500 at a pinch, but it was scarcely designed for comfort. The female members of the audience sat opposite each other in rows of seats arranged at right angles to the stage – 'as if in an omnibus', according to Clara Novello, the daughter of Mendelssohn's English publisher – while the men crushed into standing room behind them wherever they could find a space. Not for nothing did the Senecan motto above the organ proclaim, 'Res severa est verum gaudium': 'True joy is a serious matter'. You really had to want to hear music to brave these conditions, and the audiences who crowded the Gewandhaus for some twenty subscription concerts each season were among the most dedicated Mendelssohn had ever encountered.

Within a few days of his arrival in Leipzig Felix had rented a second-floor flat in one of the city's most sought-after districts, relishing the morning sunlight that flooded his elegant pair of rooms. As he reported to Abraham, he felt so 'assiduous and domesticated' that he was getting up at seven o'clock each morning and was at his desk composing by eight. His music was already well known in the city – the *Midsummer Night's Dream, Calm Sea and Prosperous Voyage* and *Hebrides* overtures had all been performed in the Gewandhaus itself – and he had several musical friends there, including Clara Wieck and the baritone Franz Hauser. Before he had even given his first Gewandhaus concert, Mendelssohn was reported by the visiting Moscheles to be 'idolised here, and lives on the most friendly terms with many musicians and notabilities, though he is intimate with but few, and reserved towards many'. Another early visitor was Chopin, to whom Mendelssohn played through his work-in-progress, *St Paul*, and who reciprocated with some of his newly composed Op. 10 Études.

Whereas in Düsseldorf Felix had found the musicians, with a few honourable exceptions, 'quite abominable', he was delighted with the professionalism and *esprit de corps* of the Gewandhaus Orchestra from the outset. His first public concert was eagerly anticipated, and when he took his place on the rostrum on 4 October the atmosphere in the hall was electric. Schumann (to whom Mendelssohn had been introduced at a Gewandhaus rehearsal the day after arriving in Leipzig) reviewed the concert with characteristic extravagance in his *Neue Zeitschrift für Musik*: 'F. Meritis [his code name for Mendelssohn] stepped out. A hundred eyes flew towards him in the first moment.' Even the relatively sober *Allgemeine Musikalische Zeitung* purpled its prose in recognition of the significance of the occasion. For Mendelssohn himself, it was the beginning of a long and mostly gratifying association, marked by mutual loyalty and responsiveness of a kind he had not experienced with any other body of musicians. 'The whole orchestra, which includes very able men, strive to guess my wishes at a glance,'

The Gewandhaus, Leipzig, 1840

he wrote to Fanny in the New Year; 'they have made the most extraordinary progress in finish and refinement, and are so devoted to me that I often feel quite moved by it.'

In the interstices of an intensely busy first season in Leipzig, Mendelssohn continued his work on *St Paul*, now in its final stages. He also completed a trio of extended but emotionally undemanding piano pieces, the earliest of them dating from July 1833, that would be published in April 1836 as the *Trois Caprices*, Op. 33; and, in almost surreal contrast with the Handelian monumentalism of the oratorio's closing choruses, revisited the fairy vein of his overture *A Midsummer Night's Dream* in the *Scherzo a capriccio* in F sharp minor for piano, dated 29 October.

Three weeks later his professional and private life was thrown into turmoil by wholly unexpected news that reached him from Berlin. On 19 November his father, whom he had last seen during a visit to Leipzigerstrasse with Moscheles in mid-October, had died after a sudden illness – probably a stroke, an affliction to which the Mendelssohns seem to have had a genetic predisposition. Felix was devastated. He returned to the family home as soon as he had found someone to stand in for him at the Gewandhaus and, writing a few days later to the Leipzig lawyer Heinrich Konrad Schleinitz about arrangements for his resumption of duties, he contrasted his own emotionalism with the self-control exhibited by Lea and his siblings: 'My family is so composed and calm that it is a consolation and an example for me; but I myself can hardly see how I shall carry on with my life.' Carry on he did, with support from his old family friend the violinist Ferdinand David, who returned to Leipzig with him after the funeral and would in February become leader of the Gewandhaus Orchestra, a post he held until his death in 1873. But Mendelssohn's sense of loss was profound. He told Klingemann that his youth ended with the day of his father's death, and his absorption in *St Paul* over the coming months was clearly, at least in part, a reflex of grief. This was, after all, a work in which Abraham had invested the highest hopes for his son, and its story of Paul's conversion, as contemporary theologians understood it, from Judaism to Christianity had a directly personal relevance for the whole Mendelssohn family.

In March 1836 Felix was awarded an honorary doctorate at the University of Leipzig in recognition of his contribution to the city's musical life, and on 18 April, after two years' attenuated work, he finally dated the score of *St Paul*. The projected first performance in Frankfurt had gone by the board because Schelble was seriously ill. (In addition to his other responsibilities, Felix agreed to stand in for Schelble at the Cäcilienverein during the summer, foregoing weeks of his precious six months' vacation to do so.) Mendelssohn had, however, been invited to direct his third Lower Rhine Music Festival in Düsseldorf in May, so he arranged for the oratorio to receive its premiere there instead, at the first of two scheduled concerts. Among the hundreds who converged on the festival by diligence and steamer were Paul Mendelssohn and his new wife Albertine, and Fanny Hensel, who sang in the chorus as she had at the previous year's festival in Cologne.

St Paul was Mendelssohn's most popular work during his lifetime, and as such has had the furthest to fall. It made a sensation at the Düsseldorf premiere on 22 May, with reviewers queuing up to proclaim it an instant classic. When performed in London the following year, it met with an unrestrained critical reception – *The Athenaeum* was typical in claiming that it should be ranked 'next to the immortal works of Handel' – and the oratorio was soon launched on an international career that saw performances as far afield as Russia and the United States. Changes in taste have made it a far less familiar presence in the modern concert hall, but even in its heyday there were critics for whom its stylistic hybridity proved a stumbling block. The deployment, in this non-liturgical context, of chorales to punctuate the episodes of the story was particularly controversial, as was one of the oratorio's most quietly effective moments of spiritual drama: the use of a four-part female chorus to represent the voice of Christ as Saul hears it on the road to Damascus. There are many such powerful moments in *St Paul* – the rapt soprano aria 'Jerusalem!' and Paul's heartfelt 'O God, have mercy' in Part 1 (Nos 7 & 18); the beautiful chorus 'Far be it from thy path!' in Part 2 (No. 42) – but some of the numbers that became popular standards in the nineteenth century, such as the pastoral chorus 'How lovely are the messengers' (No. 26), now seem to sail dangerously close to the wind of sentimentality. Most damaging of all, perhaps, is the work's dramatic top-heaviness. Most of the 'action' – the stoning of Stephen, Saul's blinding revelation, the miraculous restoration of his sight and his subsequent baptism – takes place in Part 1, and Part 2, which deals with three episodes in the apostle's ministry, culminating in his departure from Ephesus, can seem anticlimactically static in comparison. Whatever its imperfections, however, *St Paul* would be displaced only by *Elijah* in the nineteenth-century pantheon of Mendelssohn's music, and for the twenty-seven-year-old Felix, unfulfilled as he remained in the field of secular dramatic work, it was central to his own self-image as a composer.

The day after the Düsseldorf premiere Mendelssohn directed a second mammoth concert, the centrepiece of which was Beethoven's Ninth Symphony. As with his first festival appearance in 1833, an additional concert was appended to the programme, at which parts of the main attraction – in this case *St Paul* – were reprised. The entire proceedings consolidated Felix's reputation both as a creative artist and as a master of ceremonies, to which role he brought that rare festival-organiser's gift for running a smooth management operation while making an audience feel like honoured personal guests. As Ferdinand Hiller observed, Mendelssohn was 'in every way the centre-point of the Festival, not only as composer, director, and pianist, but also as a lively and agreeable host'.

The composer too saw the event as setting the seal on a new phase in his career. 'I have now probably established myself firmly in Germany,' he wrote to his mother on 1 June 1836, a few days before he left Düsseldorf for Frankfurt, 'and will not have to wander abroad to make a living. This has been clearly evident only for a year – namely, since my position in Leipzig – but I certainly believe that it is so.' Around the same time, he was offered the directorship of the Frankfurt Cäcilienverein on a permanent basis, but turned it down in favour of renewing his Leipzig contract for another year.

A new era was about to begin in his personal life, too. He had stopped over in Frankfurt on his way to Düsseldorf in early May, and it was there, on the fourth day of the month, that his eye had been caught by one of the singers in the Cäcilienverein chorus. Cécile-Sophie-Charlotte Jeanrenaud was eighteen years old and strikingly attractive, somewhat after the manner of a Dickens heroine. 'Her figure was slight,' the soprano Elise Polko later recalled,

> of middle height, and rather drooping, like a flower heavy
> with dew, her luxuriant golden-brown hair fell in rich curls
> on her shoulders, her complexion was of transparent delicacy,
> her smile charming, and she had the most bewitching deep
> blue eyes I ever beheld, with dark eyelashes and eyebrows.

She was also, as Mendelssohn discovered when he began to see more of her on his return to Frankfurt after the festival, an accomplished painter and schooled in all the graces of the aristocratic drawing room. Cécile's father, a pastor in the French Reformed Church, came from a prominent Huguenot family. When he died his daughter was just two years old, so she and her two surviving siblings were brought up by their mother's patrician family, the Souchays, under the stern eye of the matriarch of the clan, Cécile's grandmother Hélène.

At first, the Frankfurt gossip was that the composer was setting his cap at the widowed Madame Jeanrenaud, a spirited forty-year-old. However, over the months during which Mendelssohn stood in for the ailing Schelble at the

Cäcilienverein, it became clear, not least to the composer himself, that it was the daughter he was really interested in. Lonely and bereft of his father's guiding spirit, Felix seems to have found in the Souchays' riverside mansion a revitalising substitute for the bustling family life of Leipzigerstrasse. At the end of June, with Cécile very much in mind, he wrote a barcarolle-like piano piece in two voices which would later appear as the sixth of his Op. 38 collection of *Songs without Words*; it would also form part of his first Christmas present to her, a priceless album that also contained autographs by Haydn, Mozart, Beethoven and Goethe. By 24 July he was writing to his sister Rebecka that he was 'dreadfully in love':

I have not an idea whether she likes me or not. But one thing is certain, that to her I owe the first real happiness I have enjoyed this year, and now for the first time I feel fresh and hopeful again.

On 9 August, after retiring with Schadow and his son to the Netherlands beach resort of Scheveningen for a pre-arranged 'bathing cure', he requested Lea's consent to a formalisation of the relationship, and exactly a month later wrote to her again with the breathless news that:

I have just become engaged to Caecilie Jeanrenaud. My head is spinning from what I have experienced today, it is already far into the night, I don't know what else to say, but I had to write to you. How rich and happy my life is.

Ten days later Felix bade farewell to his fiancée and returned to Leipzig to launch his second concert season, one of the highlights of which was a groundbreaking authentic realisation (with organ continuo instead of the wind

The composer's wife Cécile Mendelsssohn (née Jeanrenaud), by Eduard Magnus

parts typically added in early nineteenth-century arrangements) of Handel's *Israel in Egypt* in the Paulinerkirche in November. The new season proved as successful as the first, and it was in the secure knowledge that his contract had been renewed for another year that Mendelssohn looked forward to his forthcoming nuptials.

Not until December, three months ahead of their wedding, did the couple make their engagement public. Felix, cryptically enough, conveyed the message at the end of his final concert of the year by improvising on Beethoven's setting of the words 'He who has a virtuous wife, may he join in our rejoicing' from the finale of *Fidelio*! During the remainder of the month he called on no fewer than 170 of his future in-laws' friends and relatives to spread the news and receive congratulations. In the depths of his depression after Abraham's death, Mendelssohn had told Schubring that, 'a new life must now begin for me, or all must be at an end'. As he celebrated Christmas 1836 with the Jeanrenauds in Frankfurt, it was clear to everyone that that new life was beginning in earnest.

Chapter 5

The Family Man
(1837–1841)

The Family Man (1837–1841)

'I am afraid that Felix's fastidiousness will prevent his getting a wife as well as a libretto,' Abraham Mendelssohn had once remarked to Eduard Devrient. On 28 March 1837 his eldest son proved at least the first of those fears unjustified.

The wedding of Felix Mendelssohn Bartholdy and Cécile Jeanrenaud was solemnised in Frankfurt at the French Reformed Church, of which both her father and her maternal great-grandfather had been pastors. According to one account, there was sufficient public interest in the occasion for chains to be stretched across the road to keep onlookers at a distance as the bride and groom took their vows, listened to the sermon (which included the double-edged reflection that this particular couple's life was unlikely to be troubled 'by the material needs and interests which govern those of most men and women') and left by carriage for a grand reception at the Souchay mansion.

The conspicuous absence of any member of Mendelssohn's immediate family at the ceremony has been the subject of much comment in biographies of the composer. His closest relative to attend was his aunt Dorothea Schlegel, now widowed and living in Frankfurt, but a woman whose undiminished vitality counted more with Felix than his mother's disapproval of their association. Relations between the Mendelssohns and the Jeanrenauds/

Souchays were certainly not of the smoothest during Felix's engagement and early married life. It was only at the Leipzig premiere of his revised version of *St Paul* on 16 March (held appropriately enough in the Paulinerkirche) that, after several failed attempts, he managed to introduce Lea to Cécile and her mother. The fact that several months passed after the wedding before Fanny and Rebecka even met their new sister-in-law also threatened to become a source of significant tension between Leipzigerstrasse and Leipzig. But there is no evidence that the Berlin Mendelssohns stayed away from the wedding with malice aforethought. After all, Lea was now sixty and in fragile health, both Rebecka and Fanny were pregnant (Fanny miscarried shortly after the ceremony), and Paul, who had followed in the family banking tradition, was in the midst of a time-consuming takeover in Hamburg. Indeed, Felix's seems to have been the only one of the Mendelssohn siblings' matrimonial choices that did *not* meet with overt parental disapproval.

The happy couple spent their wedding night in Mainz at the fashionable Rheinischer Hof hotel before leaving on their honeymoon journey – 'without any specific plan,' Felix wrote to Lea, 'except being happy' – in a fine new brown and blue carriage Mendelssohn had bought for the purpose. During their meandering travels through the Rhineland (and for several months after they returned home in the middle of May) Felix and Cécile kept a joint diary in which they recorded their impressions, encounters, pastimes, moods and ailments. Largely written by Cécile, with interpolations and pen-and-ink drawings by Felix, it is a document of charming immediacy that opens a brief but invaluable window onto the Mendelssohns' daily married life, of which it is the only detailed first-hand account. The young couple who emerge from its pages are uncomplicatedly happy in each other's company and in their erotic life – Cécile's entry for 29 March complains of the cold and comfortless inn where they stayed in Worms, but concludes, 'There was, however, one agreeable thing which I will refrain from mentioning!' Fretful when separated, they are also the centre of a bewilderingly populous orbit of friends, family and admirers.

Despite the omnipresence of musicians and artists in their social circle, there is scarcely a whiff of Bohemia in their daily life together. Indeed, its keynote, as mediated through the slightly Pooterish voice of Cécile, is precisely that Biedermeier respectability from which posthumous assessments of Mendelssohn have never quite succeeded in distancing him. He is a whirlwind of unremitting activity – physical, social, professional, creative – capable, at least at this stage, of bouncing back quickly from the inevitable periods of tiredness and low spirits engendered by his punishing routine. There is an appealing puckishness in his subversion of the public expectations to which he is so continuously exposed, as when he gives a false name at the town gate in Karlsruhe in order not to have to do the rounds of its musicians. His sense of humour, too, seems far less dated in pictures than in words. When Cécile has a troublesome molar extracted, for instance, he sketches the offending tooth – human-sized – lying on its side under the sculptured arch of a grand memorial. But both he and Cécile are also unquestioning prisoners of their birthright, furious when waiters fall short of acceptable standards, and given to portraying the lower orders as comic relief when not cancelling reservations to avoid having to share hotel dining rooms with them.

The composer's attentiveness to his new wife is unquestionably heartfelt; but even here the diary hints at more than a streak of his father's conventionality. In an entry richly suggestive of the dynamics and preconceptions of the Mendelssohns' domestic life, Cécile writes on Saturday 22 April:

Felix spent the afternoon composing. (In connection with which, it is from now on to be understood that I also do things, which, however, are so unimportant and not worth relating, that I need not remind myself of any of them.)

To which her husband appends the banteringly legalistic codicil:

Formal protest, which wishes to be included in the text. 'In so far as it is not unimportant and even less unworthy of being related, that holes be darned and a man go out no more ragged than his wife, then it must also be gratefully acknowledged by the former that it is in this way that his outward appearance is patched and otherwise improved… This… has more lasting worth than a good many contrapuntal twists and devices.'

Mendelssohn's protracted bachelorhood had also left him with an incurable habit of flirtation, which caused the odd tiff even during the honeymoon. But for all its surface tensions, there can be little doubt that the Mendelssohns' marriage was a happy and fulfilling one for both partners. The union would produce five children over the next eight years, and it furnished the constitutionally restless composer with a stable family environment for the first time since he left Leipzigerstrasse on his grand tour of Europe eight years earlier.

Mendelssohn's relationship with Cécile seems to have acted as a spur to his creative life, too. In January 1837 he completed two collections of works for publication by

Breitkopf & Härtel: the Six Songs (*Sechs Gesänge*), Op. 34, and the Six Preludes and Fugues for piano, Op. 35. Two of the Six Songs were written after he met Cécile – No. 4, 'Suleika' (a setting of a poem he believed to be by Goethe, but which is actually by Marianne von Willemer) and No. 6, 'Reiselied' – while the choice of the others and their dedication to his new sister-in-law Julie are clearly informed by his new circumstances. The Op. 34 set includes what is probably Mendelssohn's most famous solo song: No. 2, a setting of Heine's 'Auf Flügeln des Gesanges' ('On Wings of Song'). Several of the Preludes and Fugues for piano had already been written, too, including the magnificent first fugue in E minor which, as we have seen, was composed as a friend lay dying in 1827; but the sixth fugue and at least three of the preludes date from the period of his engagement, as do the three posthumously published preludes, Op. 104a (presumably discards from the Op. 35 set). One of Mendelssohn's most distinguished contributions to the literature of the piano, the Preludes and Fugues seem in part to have been conceived as an antidote to the salon elegance of the *Songs without Words*. Despite Schumann's observation that they have 'much of Sebastian' about them, however, these are far from being the keyboard equivalent of a historical re-enactment. The form may owe its origins to *The Well-tempered Clavier*, but no one could realistically mistake these preludes and fugues for the work of Bach. Only one of the preludes, No. 2, makes a bow in the direction of the Baroque, while No. 3 could easily be one of Mendelssohn's elfin scherzos, and Nos 5 and 6 belong recognisably to the same world as the *Songs without Words*. Even the fugues are clearly of the nineteenth rather than the eighteenth century. Unlike the *Seven Characteristic Pieces*, where the Baroque and the early Romantic sit side by side without talking, Op. 35 is a genuine conversation of old

Mendelssohn's characteristically meticulous autograph of 'Auf Flügeln des Gesanges' ('On Wings of Song')

and new, and represents Mendelssohn's capacity, in his finest work, for assimilating historical forms and disciplines to the idioms of modernity.

Other keyboard works followed on the honeymoon itself. In four days at the beginning of April Felix composed three pieces for organ, which became the preludes of the

Three Preludes and Fugues, Op. 37, published later in the year with a dedication to his old English friend Thomas Attwood (the fugues date from 1834, 1836 and 1833 respectively). The collection represents a similar enterprise in historical assimilation to the Preludes and Fugues for piano, Op. 35: 'Me voilà perruqué' ('See me in my wig'), Mendelssohn remarked in a letter to Hiller. Despite his self-deprecation, however, Op. 37 is Mendelssohn's first major contribution to the literature of the organ and arguably the most important by any composer since the death of Bach.

On 22 April Felix presented Cécile with a little *Allegretto* in A major for piano (together with a bouquet of violets, once interleaved with the honeymoon diary and still preserved in the Bodleian Library in Oxford). He also organised for publication a third set of *Songs without Words*, which would appear as his Op. 38 later in the year. The last song of the set to be composed, No. 5 in A minor, was finished in Speyer on 5 April, the same day Cécile recorded in their honeymoon diary that 'Felix played the organ of an atrociously decorated church – a wretched box of whistles'. Unlike the previous two sets, the Op. 38 collection finishes not with a Venetian 'Gondellied' but with the affectionate 'Duet without words' that Felix had included in Cécile's Christmas autograph album. (A piano 'Gondellied' in A major, composed on 5 February 1837, remained uncollected.) The whole collection was dedicated to Rosa von Woringen, the sister of the dedicatee of Mendelssohn's Op. 30 set. There are indications, though, that the composer was already beginning to feel some ambivalence towards the genre he had invented. 'I won't publish any more very soon,' he wrote to Fanny a few days before he sent off Op. 38 to the publisher; 'I would rather write bigger things.'

Before he and Cécile returned from their honeymoon on 15 May he had put his resolution into effect, making a start on three major works: the String Quartet in E minor (later to be published as Op. 44 No. 2), his first since the Quartet in E flat major of 1829; a setting of Psalm 42 as a concert cantata for solo voices, choir, orchestra and organ (Op. 42); and the Piano Concerto No. 2 in D minor (Op. 40). It would be four years before he published his next set of *Songs without Words*, Op. 53. There was no let-up in his creative buoyancy when the couple got back to Frankfurt, where Felix found waiting for him the published copies of the Six Songs, Op. 34 and the Preludes and Fugues, Op. 35. A fortnight later he wrote to his mother:

> *I really could not have imagined that I would ever be so completely happy in my life, and now I am. It is such a blissful time for my life and my art that I never know how to thank God enough for it, with musical thoughts and work in abundance for my new pieces, while the old ones are making all the impression I could wish for. My 'St Paul' has been performed here twice in a week to full houses… and I may hope that one of these days I will write something that will approach what I would always so dearly like to express, and only so rarely can…*

His principal focus was the three works he had begun on his honeymoon. The String Quartet in E minor (known unchronologically as No. 4) was written out by 18 June, shortly after the couple decamped to Krontal – the scene of their engagement – to escape disruptive building work on the Souchay mansion. The setting of Psalm 42 followed in July, and by the end of that month a new string quartet in

E flat (the future Op. 44 No. 3) was also all but complete in Mendelssohn's head, as was the motet *Laudate pueri* for female chorus and organ, which would join the two Roman motets *Veni, Domine* and *Surrexit Pastor* as the Three Motets, Op. 39, when they were published in 1838. In April Felix had accepted an invitation to conduct at the Birmingham Music Festival in September. *St Paul* would be the central work of the four-day festival, but he also wanted to present his new piano concerto, of which, he wrote to Lea on 13 July, 'not a single note... is yet written down'. Eleven days later, in a letter from Bingen (where they had gone for a four-week summer holiday with Felix's mother- and sister-in-law), Cécile describes to Rebecka how her husband is hard at work on the concerto in the same room:

> He sits facing me trilling with his fingers, writing, singing, blowing the trumpet and flute, all at the same time; then he walks up and down the room again with his sheet of music, beating time or playing the double bass with his arm...

The original plan had been for Felix and Cécile to travel to England together for the festival – he had been giving her some rather earnest English lessons during their honeymoon – but at the beginning of June it became clear that she was pregnant, and a long journey was considered inadvisable. It was therefore a solitary Felix who waved goodbye to his wife of five months as his steamer pulled away from the Düsseldorf quayside on 24 August 1837 at the start of what would prove yet another of his stormy passages to England.

Cécile continued to write the couple's diary until her husband's return at the end of September, while Felix kept detailed notes and wrote them up much later for insertion in the diary as a parallel day-to-day account of his experiences during their separation. The effect is rather like watching a split-screen film: one side of each daily entry shows Cécile pursuing the humdrum daily life of a patrician *Hausfrau*, her scope for action increasingly limited by her pregnancy; the other shows a man plunging into the dizzying maelstrom of social and musical activity which was by now the natural element of his celebrity.

Mendelssohn's fifth tour of England was another triumphal progress. He arrived on 27 August to see the faithful Klingemann rowing across the Thames to greet him, and made a sketch of the Thames-side buildings for Cécile. (Prominent on a wall in the foreground is the legend 'Warren's Blacking' – the factory where Charles Dickens, now the son-in-law of Felix's old Edinburgh friend George Hogarth, had worked so bitterly as a child a few years earlier.) Within hours Mendelssohn had re-established contact with Friedrich Rosen, the Horsleys, Novello and other London friends and acquaintances. Almost immediately, too, he found himself embroiled in an ugly controversy with his principal hosts, the Birmingham Music Festival committee. An amateur working-class music society, the Sacred Harmonic Society, had also asked him to conduct a performance of *St Paul* at Exeter Hall in London, and he had agreed. Birmingham, however, regarded their festival arrangement as exclusive and insisted he withdraw from the London engagement. Mendelssohn grudgingly conceded, but the Birmingham authorities then tried to get the Exeter Hall performance cancelled altogether, and for days afterwards the disagreement rumbled on acrimoniously in the pages of the public press. The composer discreetly attended the Exeter Hall rehearsals, only to be recognised, at which point, *tremendous yelling, rejoicing, calls for three cheers and hat waving broke out, lasting several minutes, so that at first I was quite alarmed and subsequently delighted at such a reception. Such a thing is unknown in Germany, where nevertheless Englishmen are termed 'the cold English'.*

At the end of the month he started work with Klingemann on the libretto for a project the two friends had discussed more than once in the preceding months – a new oratorio on the subject of the Old Testament prophet Elijah. (The Klingemann collaboration came to nothing on this occasion, and subsequent discussions with Julius Schubring ran into the sand in 1839 when Mendelssohn found himself too busy to take them forward; not until 1845 did he return to the project.) At the beginning of September he wrote out the piano part of his new concerto. He also attended evensong at St Paul's, where he played the organ after the service had ended. A crowd of people gathered in the Cathedral to listen, only for the organ to go dead on him as he was coming to the end of Bach's Prelude and Fugue in A minor, BWV 543. As Mendelssohn tells it in his diary entry for 10 September: 'the organ-blower, on instructions from the beadle, who had not been able to get anybody to leave the church and had been obliged to stay on longer against his will, had left the bellows, locked the door to them, and departed'! He was amused by the near-riot that ensued among the spectators and (at least until he got sick of being asked about it at every turn) by the fact that the story found its way into not just the national but the international press.

On the evening of 12 September he attended the Exeter Hall performance of *St Paul* – it was, he recorded, 'singularly interesting for me, since I <u>heard</u> my oratorio for the first time'. The end of the first part was greeted by 'the greatest burst of applause that I had yet heard in my life; the whole audience to a man stood up and turned round in my direction. When he got up to take a bow, people waved their hats and handkerchiefs and stood on the seats shouting his name, and several friends he thought were abroad came up to congratulate him. At the end of the performance there was another ecstatic ovation. But tragedy followed hard on the heels of triumph. Ever since Mendelssohn had arrived in London, Friedrich Rosen's health had been giving cause for concern, and the very morning of the concert he had been diagnosed with advanced cancer. Mendelssohn drove to Rosen's house after the performance, only to meet Klingemann coming down the stairs, looking 'pale and bewildered; Rosen had died in his arms while the jubilation was going on in the hall'.

The next morning, his mind still churning from the incomprehensible events of the night before, Mendelssohn took the coach to Birmingham, where he arrived at half past six in the evening to learn that he would have only one day of rehearsals for the four days and seven performances of the festival. Despite these testing conditions, his contributions to the proceedings were as enthusiastically received as he could have wished. He conducted *St Paul* on the second day, and gave the premiere of his new piano concerto on the third, by which time he was too exhausted to accede to the audience's demands for an encore of the finale.

Like the first concerto, the Piano Concerto No. 2 in D minor, Op. 40 is in three connected movements and features much virtuosic writing, especially in the outer movements. It lacks something of the conviction that propels its predecessor, however, and it has never achieved the same popularity with either performers or audiences. Mendelssohn himself was often disparaging about the Concerto, writing to Lea, for example, that it was 'nothing very special as a composition, but the last movement creates so much effect as a piece of pianistic pyrotechnics that I often have to laugh when I happen to play it properly'. Schumann, speculating that it must have been written in a few days, if not a few hours, wrote: 'This concerto belongs to his most casual products... So let us enjoy this bright, unpretentious gift; it is like one of those works we know from the old masters done when they are resting from their more important labours'. Mendelssohn would take this Concerto on the road to great acclaim in the years ahead, but Schumann's judgement has remained, by and large, the verdict of posterity.

His life meticulously scheduled, as always, Mendelssohn made his last festival appearance at the organ in Bach's Prelude and Fugue in E flat, BWV 552 with a carriage already waiting at the door to whisk him down to London. From there, he left at midnight for Dover, where he had his usual bad luck in the Channel, his steamer being redirected from Calais to Boulogne because of stormy weather. Five days of continuous travelling later, he arrived back in Frankfurt: 'my journey and the separation were at an end,' he wrote, 'and I joyfully embraced my dearest Cécile once again'. They are the last words of the Mendelssohns' honeymoon diary.

The very next day after Felix's return he and Cécile left Frankfurt for Leipzig, where they arrived on 1 October, just in time for him to conduct the opening concert of his third season at the Gewandhaus. No wonder Fanny, in a letter to Cécile of 5 October, expressed concern at the frantic pace of Felix's professional life – 'this eternal mad rush in which he lives year in and year out'. The same letter also gives vent to some irritation at the delay in meeting Cécile face to face: 'when anybody comes to talk to me about your beauty and your eyes,' Fanny wrote, 'it makes me quite cross. I have had enough of hearsay, and beautiful eyes were not meant to be heard.' A few days later, the Hensels arrived in Leipzig and, more than a year after Mendelssohn announced his engagement, the two most important women in his life finally met one another. Fanny was favourably impressed both with Cécile's self-evident love for her brother and with her management of his moods: 'she does not spoil him,' she wrote to Klingemann, 'but when he is capricious treats him with an equanimity which will in course of time most likely cure his fits of irritability altogether.' The ice was well and truly broken, no doubt to the relief of all concerned, though it would be another six months before Felix introduced his wife to Rebecka.

In what was by now establishing itself as the regular pattern of his professional life, Mendelssohn's Gewandhaus season effectively displaced new composition to the spring and summer months. The 1837–8 season was a typically busy one, during which, in addition to the usual crowded concert schedule, the Mendelssohns had to arrange accommodation for themselves in Leipzig. (After living for a while in the same block as one of Cécile's elderly relatives, they moved into their own flat in the Lurgensteins Garten, an airy second-floor apartment with views over gardens, fields and St Thomas's Church and School.) The new season featured the Leipzig premiere of the Second Piano Concerto, with the composer himself at the keyboard, and an innovative series of 'historical concerts' at which, in a public echo of his last meetings with Goethe in 1830, Mendelssohn presented works from the Baroque to the present in chronological progression – an exercise which, for all its apparent artificiality, has been seen as a significant moment in the formation of a European musical canon. He also pursued his unending search for a workable opera subject: protracted discussions with James Robinson Planché, the London-based librettist of Weber's

Oberon, came to nothing, depriving posterity of a (not easily imaginable) Mendelssohnian take on Edward III's siege of Calais. In addition, he prepared for publication his six songs *Im Freien zu singen* ('For Singing Out of Doors') for mixed voices, Op. 41. The first of a tetralogy of part-song collections that would be published over the next few years, these were intended for social performances such as those Mendelssohn and his friends indulged in during picnics in the woods around Frankfurt. All four collections found an appreciative market among the music-loving public of his time, several of the numbers acquiring something of the status of folksongs. More significantly, by December he had also revised his setting of Psalm 42, which was premiered on 1 January 1838 with Clara Novello, the current darling of the Gewandhaus audience, as soprano soloist. The text of the psalm is 'As the hart panteth after the water brooks, so panteth my soul after thee, O God'. There is little of spiritual striving about the setting, however, which seems rather to express the composer's newfound domestic happiness. Perhaps for this very reason, the Psalm, which was one of Mendelssohn's most-performed sacred works during his lifetime – Schumann went so far as to declare it the ideal template for all contemporary church music – has sharply declined in popularity since his death.

Another work conceived before the beginning of the concert season and committed to paper during gaps in Mendelssohn's performing and administrative programme was the String Quartet in E flat major, Op. 44 No. 3, the score of which is dated 6 February 1838. The very next day Cécile gave birth to the Mendelssohns' first child, whom they named Carl Wolfgang Paul. By the beginning of April Mendelssohn had composed two occasional pieces: for the birthday of the Austrian Emperor Ferdinand I a *Festgesang* for chorus and piano (the theme of which sounds like a dry run for the opening motto of the *Lobgesang* Symphony of 1840); and for the last concert of the season a *Serenade and Allegro giojoso* for piano and orchestra, Op. 43, which is less notable for its musical content than for its having been tossed off in two days flat. Shortly after performing the latter Mendelssohn finished work on another psalm setting, this time of Psalm 95; though only in 1842, after much revision, was he happy to usher it into print as his Op. 46.

Felix, Cécile and Carl spent the summer with the Berlin Mendelssohns at 3 Leipzigerstrasse, from which the male members of the clan were absent at intervals in pursuit of their various callings: Paul in Hamburg on banking business; Wilhelm Hensel in London exercising his pencil at the coronation of the nineteen-year-old Queen Victoria; and Felix in Cologne directing the twentieth Lower Rhine Music Festival at the end of May. To this summer belong a spirited three-movement Violin Sonata in F major (which only resurfaced in the 1950s, having been set aside in dissatisfaction), and the first stirrings of what would much later become the Violin Concerto in E minor, as well as of the 'Lobgesang' Symphony and the Cello Sonata No. 1. Towards the end of July Mendelssohn also completed the third (in order of composition) of the string quartets that would be published together the following year as his Op. 44: the String Quartet in D major.

The Op. 44 quartets are the central works of Mendelssohn's early married life and among his most sustained achievements in chamber music. All three quartets bear witness to a renewed engagement with Classical forms and to his lifelong concern for what he called 'clarity' of musical expression. Whereas his two earlier numbered quartets spoke, to a greater or lesser extent, the dislocated language of late Beethoven, the Op. 44 works are characterised by their thematic unity and homogeneity of affect. The mood of the E minor Quartet (No. 2 of the set, but the first to be written) has often been likened to that of the Violin Concerto, Op. 64, with which it shares its key and the elegiac contours of its opening subject. The third movement is a radiantly songlike *Andante*, in marked contrast to the yearning *Adagio non troppo* of the E flat major Quartet (No. 3 of the set, but the second to be written). The E flat major Quartet also features a scurrying dust-storm of a scherzo which is among Mendelssohn's most original contributions to the form. The D major Quartet (No. 1), apparently the composer's favourite of the set, has one of the most exuberant openings of any of his chamber works, in which one seems to hear the overflowing happiness that his contemporary letters speak of so eloquently. The second movement is a very Classical minuet, whose haunting trio returns briefly to conclude the movement. The Op. 44 quartets are dedicated to the crown prince of Sweden, whom Mendelssohn had met shortly after his return from honeymoon.

Felix, Cécile and Carl cut short their Berlin visit in August when a measles epidemic swept the Prussian capital. The six-month-old Carl escaped infection, but Rebecka's baby son Felix was not so lucky, and died in November. By then his uncle and namesake, having recovered from a bout of the measles himself, was submerged in perhaps the most memorable of all his Leipzig seasons, the climax of which took place on 21 March 1839. It was then that Mendelssohn introduced to the Gewandhaus audience, and to the world, a work that had lain undiscovered for more than ten years since its composer's death: Franz Schubert's last symphony, the 'Great' C major, D. 944. It was Schumann who had unearthed the score while looking through manuscripts in Schubert's brother's flat in Vienna in 1838, and it was he who brought it to Felix's attention. But it was Mendelssohn's electrifying performance that launched it on its career as a perennial of the symphonic repertoire. At a stroke, his premiere of the Symphony revolutionised Schubert's reputation for the nineteenth century and beyond in much the same way that his revival of the *St Matthew Passion* had revolutionised Bach's a decade earlier. Schumann wrote of the Symphony's 'heavenly length', and the great conductor Hans von Bülow, who took piano lessons from Mendelssohn as a boy, never forgot the excitement of hearing one of the master's dozen performances of it:

> At that time it was not yet fashionable to install Schubert on the heights of Mt Olympus; he was loved, admired, and enjoyed as a minorum gentium, but there were complaints about the expansiveness of his forms and the monotony of his rhythms. But under Mendelssohn's baton, one was not aware of these faults... For we had just dwelt in eternity in a timeless world.

On the programme at the same 21 March concert was a new work of Mendelssohn's own which, despite its unpromising title on that occasion – 'Overture for the Theatre Pension Fund'! – has also established itself as a standard of the modern concert hall. The overture *Ruy Blas*, posthumously published as Op. 95, was commissioned for a charity performance of Victor Hugo's play of the same name at the Leipzig theatre. Ironically, Mendelssohn heartily disliked the play and was initially reluctant to contribute more than an incidental Romance for female voices and strings, posthumously published as the vocal duet Op. 77 No. 3. When he finally persuaded himself to accept, however, he composed the overture in just three days, leaving only another three days before the premiere. Despite this timetable, the music itself shows no signs of haste, and while it has no pretensions to the status of Mendelssohn's three great concert overtures, its beguiling mixture of (mock?-) solemnity and swagger has assured it a place in the repertoire long after Hugo's play has become a historical curiosity.

As in the previous year, Mendelssohn's professional engagements continued after the end of the Gewandhaus season with the direction of the Lower Rhine Music Festival. His leadership had by now helped to elevate this event to one of Germany's most talked-about musical gatherings. Held in Düsseldorf between 19 and 21 May, the twenty-first festival featured Handel's *Messiah* on the programme of its opening concert and also saw performances of Mendelssohn's Psalm 42 and Second Piano Concerto.

If the composer was wearied by this relentless schedule, he showed no signs of it back in Frankfurt, where he spent the summer in the social, musical and creative ferment that passed for holiday in the Mendelssohn household. In addition to three organ fugues (one of which would later be remarshalled in the Organ Sonata, Op. 65 No. 2) he

completed on 18 July the Piano Trio in D minor, Op. 49, the first of his two mature works for this combination of players. One of the greatest of all Mendelssohn's chamber compositions, the four-movement trio is the creation of a composer at the height of his powers, in complete command of his material and means of expression. The work's formal balance and breadth of melodic invention led Schumann to describe it as 'the trio masterpiece of the present time' and to hail Mendelssohn as 'the Mozart of the nineteenth century'. Likewise, Ferdinand Hiller apostrophised the trio's 'fire and spirit, the flow, and, in short, the masterly character of the whole thing'. (He also claimed to have persuaded Mendelssohn to update his original keyboard writing to reflect the more flamboyant pianism made fashionable by Chopin and Liszt.) Mendelssohn's own assessment of the work, by contrast, was typically level-headed: 'I really enjoy that piece,' Hiller reports him as saying; 'it is honest music after all, and the players will like it, because they can show off with it.'

Characteristic of Mendelssohn's lifelong ability to create radically different works concurrently or in close succession is his monumental setting of Psalm 114, Op. 51, written immediately after the Piano Trio and completed by 9 August. Equally characteristic of the pattern of Mendelssohn's life, however, is what looks increasingly like an inability to say no to professional engagements. Invitations were multiplying as his reputation grew, and he knew he was spreading himself thin. As early as his return from the Birmingham Music Festival in 1837 he had recognised the challenge presented by the proliferating demands on his time and attention, musing to his brother Paul:

So few traces remain of performances and music festivals, and all that is personal; the people indeed shout and applaud, but that quickly passes away, without leaving a vestige behind, and yet it absorbs as much of one's life and strength as better things, or perhaps even more; and the evil of this is, that it is impracticable to come half out, when you are once in; you must either go on the whole way, or not at all. I dare not even attempt to withdraw, or the cause I have undertaken will suffer... I long for a less busy life, in order to be able to devote myself to my peculiar province, composition of music, and to leave the execution of it to others.

137

As he embarked, with self-evident joy, on his own family life with Cécile, such competing responsibilities must have looked less mutually compatible than ever. Nonetheless, after the rigours of the autumn and winter at the Gewandhaus, followed by the major task of directing the Lower Rhine Music Festival in May, Mendelssohn agreed to lead yet another music festival – this time in Brunswick in Saxony – less than a month before resuming his duties in Leipzig. Thus at the end of August 1839 he returned to Saxony to a hero's welcome and three days of concerts, the first of which featured his own *St Paul*. Mendelssohn had also agreed to conduct the oratorio at a concert of Vienna's Gesellschaft der Musikfreunde, which had made him an honorary member in 1837, but in the event he withdrew after a bitter public disagreement about his expenses for the trip. Then on 2 October, just four days before the start of the new Gewandhaus season, Cécile gave birth to the Mendelssohns' second child, Marie Pauline Hélène. The events of the next few months – which included a vigorous and ultimately successful campaign to increase his musicians' salaries – were thus played out against the backdrop of a household dominated by the needs of two children under the age of two, in whose upbringing Mendelssohn played a proud and active part. Eric Werner, whose biography of the composer revitalised Mendelssohn studies in the early 1960s, asked at the end of his chapter on Felix's marriage: 'Is it not sad that the creative spirit had to pay for his private, innocent joy as a human being with a diminution in the value of his achievement?' Whatever the effect on Mendelssohn's creative life of his embrace of domesticity, however, one hardly needs the pram-in-the-hall theory to account for any decline in his output, at least in terms of quantity, from the mid-1830s. As far as the pace of his daily life was concerned, these were

p.154

unequivocally not, in the title of Werner's chapter on the period 1837–1841, 'The Tranquil Years'. Now more than ever Mendelssohn simply didn't do tranquil.

As in 1838–9, the most spectacular event of the 1839–40 season was reserved until the end, when Franz Liszt made his first appearance at the Gewandhaus. If not yet the heart-throb superstar he would become the following year, when his flamboyant concert tour of Berlin led Heine to coin the term 'Lisztmania', at twenty-eight years old Liszt was still the most brilliant piano virtuoso of his time. As Mendelssohn reported to Fanny, however, his two-week visit 'caused a devil of a scandal'. Cashing in on his client's celebrity, Liszt's agent had ratcheted up the ticket prices for the recitals, and there was some booing when the virtuoso first glided onto the platform on 17 March. His performance, too, sharply divided opinion. Hiller recalled how half the public stood on their seats when Liszt played Schubert's *Erlkönig*, but that his ambitious piano transcription of movements from Beethoven's 'Pastoral' Symphony sounded bloodless and inappropriate 'in a hall where it had been heard so often in its variegated orchestral garb'. Over the years Mendelssohn had warmed to Liszt both as a pianist and as a man, though he lamented the high-handed PR of what he called this 'novel apparition, the virtuoso of the nineteenth century'. Ever the professional host, however, he soothed his guest's ruffled feathers by laying on, before Liszt's second concert appearance,

> *a soirée for 350 people in the Gewandhaus, with orchestra, chorus, bishop, cake,* Meerestille, *Psalm [42], Bach's Triple Concerto (Liszt, Hiller, and me), choruses from* St Paul, *fantasy on* Lucia di Lammermoor, Erlkönig, *the devil and his grandmother!*

Schumann described the occasion, as 'three joyous hours of music such as one does not experience otherwise for years at a time.'

Liszt's visit furnished another spectacular example of Mendelssohn's barely credible musical memory. One of those present at a musical gathering *chez* Mendelssohn was the philologist F. Max Müller, whose father was the poet of Schubert's great song cycles *Die schöne Müllerin* and *Winterreise*. Müller recalled:

> Liszt appeared in his Hungarian costume, wild and magnificent. He told Mendelssohn that he had written something special for him. He sat down, and swaying right and left on his music-stool, played first a Hungarian melody, and then three or four variations, one more incredible than the other.

Urged to play something in return, Mendelssohn at first demurred, then conceded with the words, 'Well, I will play but you must not get angry with me.' He then proceeded to reproduce, note for note, the folksong and variations he had just heard. Müller continues:

> We all trembled lest Liszt should be offended, for Mendelssohn could not keep himself from slightly imitating Liszt's movements and raptures. However, Mendelssohn managed never to offend man, woman, or child. Liszt laughed and applauded, and admitted that no one, not even he himself, could have performed such a bravura...

No sooner was the concert season over than Mendelssohn began another of his campaigns, this time for the formation of a music conservatoire in Leipzig. Around the same time he seems to have had his final falling-out with A.B. Marx, the mentor of his youth, with whom relations had been cooling for some time. Apparently, Marx showed Mendelssohn the score of his cherished oratorio *Mose*, probably on a visit to Leipzig in April 1840; when Mendelssohn declined to promote it, he returned huffily to Berlin, threw his old friend's letters into the river, and began a bitter critical campaign against him in the musical press.

The following month Mendelssohn conducted *St Paul* in Weimar, and in June took part in Leipzig's three-day Gutenberg Festival, a celebration of the 400th anniversary of the invention of the printing press. Mendelssohn's contributions to the proceedings were twofold. First, he composed a *Festgesang* for male chorus and double brass band, which was performed to great effect in the market square on the second day of the festival (24 June). Unremembered in its original form, the work would achieve an unlikely afterlife when, nine years after Mendelssohn's death, an English organist by the name of William Cummings noticed that the words of Charles Wesley's Christmas carol *Hark! the herald angels sing* would fit the rousing tune of its second movement.

Mendelssohn's second contribution to the Gutenberg Festival has been less gratefully received by posterity. On 25 June, in the hallowed surroundings of St Thomas's, he premiered his *Lobgesang* ('Hymn of Praise'), published as Op. 52 and now known as his Symphony No. 2. Mendelssohn later adopted, at Klingemann's suggestion, the subtitle 'Symphony-Cantata', and, as the designation implies, the *Lobgesang* is a hybrid work, combining three opening orchestral movements with nine choral movements. As a species of choral symphony, it has always invited comparisons with Beethoven's Ninth, inevitably to its own disadvantage. It is, however, a very different work from Beethoven's in several respects. For one thing, the texts Mendelssohn chose for the choral sections are biblical in origin – mostly from the Psalms – and the *Lobgesang* thus bridges the secular and the religious realm. Mendelssohn further binds the instrumental and choral sections together by introducing vocal elements into the former – a recitative for clarinet links the first two movements, and the trio of the second movement features an original chorale – and by introducing and concluding the cantata with the majestic motto theme that opens the whole work. Despite this unity of intention and effect, however, the *Lobgesang*'s fundamental heterogeneity militates against sustained focus, and it remains the most problematic and the least heard of Mendelssohn's five mature symphonies.

The bunting had hardly been taken down after the Gutenberg celebrations before Mendelssohn set off for the next in his seemingly endless round of festivals. This time it was the North German Musical Festival, held in Schwerin in Mecklenburg, where he conducted *St Paul* and Haydn's *Creation* and took to the dance floor with his customary disdain for half measures at a grand ball thrown in his honour. Returning to Leipzig via Berlin, he immediately flung himself into preparations for a solo recital of Bach's organ works at St Thomas's on 6 August – part of his fundraising campaign to erect a monument to the former Thomaskantor outside the Thomasschule itself. (The statue was unveiled in 1843 in the presence of Bach's only surviving grandson.) Four days after the concert he told Lea he had practised the pedal parts so assiduously that he could 'hardly stand upright any more, and walked down the street in nothing but organ passages'. The physical effects of all this frenetic activity ran deeper than he thought, however. In the summer of 1837 he had apparently got into serious difficulties while swimming in the Rhine. Now once again he was taken ill while swimming, and was unconscious and convulsed for some hours in what

Robert and Clara
Schumann, 1850

seems likely, despite his relative youth, to have been a stroke. Nonetheless he insisted, against the advice of his doctors, on keeping his commitment to conduct at the Birmingham Music Festival at the end of the month. Arriving in London on 17 September, he spent a couple of days with old friends before taking the new railway up to Birmingham, where he conducted the *Lobgesang*, performed his First Piano Concerto and played the organ at the Town Hall. The *Lobgesang* Symphony made a profound impression, all in the audience rising to their feet when the not obviously climactic chorale

'Nun danket alle Gott' ('Now thank we all our God') struck up (No. 8) – 'a custom', as Moscheles reported, 'usually confined in England to the performance of the Hallelujah Chorus'.

By 9 October Mendelssohn was back in Leipzig, and the new Gewandhaus season was underway. The highlights of his schedule over the next six months included another performance of Bach's Triple Concerto in D minor (this time with Moscheles and the newly married Clara Schumann) and the composition of the *Allegro brillant* for piano duet, Op. 92, for the debut of Clara with her husband Robert. He also introduced to the Gewandhaus the Norwegian violinist Ole Bull (with whom he performed Beethoven's 'Kreutzer' Sonata) and gave the premiere of Schumann's First Symphony, the 'Spring'. In addition, he conducted the *St Matthew Passion* for the last time (in St Thomas's, where it had first been heard more than a century earlier), restoring in the process some of the cuts he had made for his famous revival of 1829.

During the first weeks of the season, Mendelssohn managed to find both time and energy to revise the *Lobgesang*, which he presented in its refurbished form at a memorable concert on 16 December. At the end of the evening, in an astounding abandonment of protocol, the King of Saxony, Frederick Augustus II, made his way to the stage through the press of auditors to congratulate Mendelssohn on his achievement. (The following July he would confer on Felix the title of Saxon Kapellmeister.) Crowning professional with domestic felicity, January saw the birth of the Mendelssohns' third child, Paul Felix Abraham (the founder, incongruously enough, of the chemical giant Agfa).

Two months later Mendelssohn was approached by Pietro Mechetti, a music publisher whom he had met in Vienna in 1830. Mechetti was putting together a volume of original compositions to help raise funds for a Beethoven memorial in Bonn, the composer's birthplace, and he invited Mendelssohn to contribute, along with Chopin, Czerny, Kalkbrenner, Liszt and Moscheles, among others. Initially unenthusiastic, by July Mendelssohn had produced for the album the composition generally seen as his masterpiece for the piano, the *Variations sérieuses*, Op. 54. The eighteen variations on an original theme of chromatic plangency are, as the name suggests, infused with a profound seriousness of intent that distinguishes them both from the often showy variations of Mendelssohn's contemporaries and from the drawing-room vein of so many of his own keyboard works. There is no gratuitous virtuosity in Mendelssohn's intense exploration of the potentialities of his theme, which reaches its emotional climax in the hymn-like stillness of the fourteenth variation, the only one in a major key. Mendelssohn seems almost to have surprised himself by how well the form suited him, and proceeded to write two more sets of piano variations, Opp. 82 and 83, 'as though I had to make up for never having written any before'. Attractive though the latter are, however, they explore less rugged terrain than Op. 54, and he never published them.

Throughout this period Mendelssohn was deeply involved in negotiations the outcome of which would have a far-reaching effect on his future life. Back in 1833, during the early days of Mendelssohn's music directorship in Düsseldorf, the visiting crown prince of Prussia had told him how much he regretted the composer's decision to leave Berlin. Acceding to the throne as Frederick William IV in June 1840, he lost little time in trying to tempt Mendelssohn back to the Prussian capital. Like a kind of royal Immermann, the monarch had grand plans for the regeneration of his territories' entire cultural life, focused on a thoroughgoing reconfiguration of Berlin's Academy of Arts into separate divisions for the individual arts. Like Immermann, too, he saw Mendelssohn as central to the whole project. The composer would, so the king vaguely hoped, run a new musical conservatoire (the embodiment of the music division of the Academy), compose sacred music and oratorios, and direct royal command performances.

Mendelssohn was wary from the first about these new and above all ill-defined responsibilities. He was inevitably dealing with Frederick William's plans at one remove, and not always the same remove at that. There was a whole tier of courtiers and ministers between him and the king, including Baron von Bunsen (with whom the plans seem to have originated), Ludwig von Massow (the under-secretary for the royal household, who was Mendelssohn's point of contact when it came to the discussion of terms and duties), and the minister Karl Friedrich Eichhorn (who as Massow's boss had responsibility for organising the proposed new conservatoire). Even the initial approach to Mendelssohn was made indirectly, through his brother Paul. This multiplicity of intermediaries was itself symptomatic of a lack of central co-ordination in the royal plans, which Mendelssohn sought to tighten up with his own detailed recommendations in May. But just as on his return from the grand tour in 1832 he had allowed himself to stand for the directorship of the Singakademie against his better judgement, so now he seemed incapable of resisting the current as it tugged him back towards involvement in the institutional life of Berlin. Happy in Leipzig and already chronically overworked, it is hardly surprising that he hesitated to return to a city about which he had distinctly mixed feelings and where, even after months of discussions, his putative job description had yet to be written. What is more surprising is that by the end of June 1841 he had apparently made up his mind to accept the latest royal offer: to move to Berlin for a year, with no clear duties beyond attendance on the king's whim, while the new conservatoire got off the ground.

Against the grain of his personality, Mendelssohn had insisted on the title Kapellmeister in order to have some formal authority over the city's musicians, none of whom had been consulted about the new arrangements; but even when this condition was thrown into doubt over the coming weeks it seemed not to change his decision. Why? In March, when he was still agonising over whether or not to accept Frederick William's original offer, Mendelssohn had written to Klingemann that the argument in favour was self-evident: 'mother and sisters and my parental home'. In the end his sense of duty to his family in Berlin, and especially to his ageing mother, outweighed all other considerations. Certainly, he knew how much his return would please them: he kept the royal approach secret to avoid getting their hopes up, and was intensely annoyed when he discovered that the court had leaked it. But apart from the ties of blood, Berlin remained, as he wrote resignedly to Klingemann on 15 July, 'one of the sourest apples one can bite, and yet it must be bitten'.

Less than a fortnight later Mendelssohn had moved back into a vacant wing of his childhood home at 3 Leipzigerstrasse with Cécile and the children. (The whole family would later take up quarters across the road.) The shaken kaleidoscope of Berlin's artistic scene had still not settled into a definitive constellation of responsibilities, but if Frederick William's plans were to be realised in anything like their ambitious original form it was clear that Mendelssohn would have his work cut out. As Bunsen had remarked of the task in prospect: 'Is that not enough for one man, one master? I believe it is rather too much for any one other than Felix Mendelssohn.' In the event, it would prove too much even for him.

Chapter 6

Serving Two Masters
(1841–1844)

> "He began immediately, & really
> I have never heard anything so
> beautiful...

Serving Two Masters (1841–1844)

Within a month of Mendelssohn's return to Berlin a new
railway line opened between Leipzig and the Prussian
capital. The train took more than eight hours to cover the
150 kilometres between the two cities, but for Mendelssohn
it was a lifeline. Uncertain what the future would bring, he
was determined not to sever his links with Leipzig. He kept
his Lurgensteins Garten flat and, when time allowed, his
Leipzig engagements, delegating the rest first to Ferdinand
David, and then, less happily, to Ferdinand Hiller (on whose
friendship the arrangement would place a terminal strain).
But the railway was also a symbol of how overstretched
Mendelssohn's lines of communication had become. For
the next three years, he would keep a foot in each of his
two principal camps, and would spend a vast amount of
his time and energy commuting between them. Not only
was it a frustratingly provisional kind of existence; he also
recognised straightaway that if he had felt alienated from
Berlin when he returned to it nearly a decade earlier, this
time he had outgrown it completely. 'I feel myself all too
estranged from this city...' he wrote to Schleinitz in Leipzig
after only a few days back in the Prussian capital. 'I feel
like arguing as soon as even an unimportant conversation
starts, I disagree so profoundly with their way of thinking...
I used to be part of them here, but now I am an outsider.'

It was a dangerous state of mind in which to open a new chapter of his professional life.

Frederick William IV had come to the Prussian throne with a weight of expectation on his shoulders. After the rigid authoritarianism of his father's reign, the Prussian people had high hopes for a more liberal regime. The auguries were good: there was some relaxation of censorship, and such formerly dissident figures as the brothers Grimm were rehabilitated and called to Berlin to participate in the restructuring of the city's cultural institutions. It soon became clear, however, that the new king's ambitions for a regeneration of Prussia's political life fell short of those for its artistic life, and that his redefinition of the bond between sovereign and subject had more to do with a romanticised neo-feudalism than with anything approaching the constitutional monarchy increasingly demanded by liberal voices in his territories and beyond. To make matters worse, Frederick William, though personally charming, was also incorrigibly indecisive – a trait of which Mendelssohn had already seen ample evidence during the long and tangled negotiations of recent months. Once resettled in Berlin, the composer thus found himself at the disposal of a king whose fatal combination of vision and vacillation was reflected in a working environment characterised by an equally fatal compound of diktat and bureaucracy. It would prove a recipe for disaster, both for Mendelssohn's immediate future and, in the longer term, for the liberal hopes of the Prussian people.

Only at the end of September, in fact, did agreement crystallise on even such basic elements of his new position as salary (at 3,000 thalers three times his Leipzig wages) and title (he got his Kapellmeistership). Around the same time, Mendelssohn received his first musical command from the

151

king. This was to compose incidental music for a revival in German translation of Sophocles' tragedy *Antigone*, the first in a projected series of classical and Shakespearean plays to be co-produced by Mendelssohn and the king's new 'chief court reader', the ageing poet and translator Ludwig Tieck. *Antigone* was in some respects a curious choice: a more imaginative monarch might have seen as potentially incendiary its exploration of the conflicting demands of authority and individual conscience. It was, however, tailor-made for the classically educated Mendelssohn, who saw in the project an opportunity to point up the enduring relevance of an ancient text with contemporary music. Indeed, he was by his own account the prime mover in the collaboration: 'the noble old style of the piece fascinated me so much,' he wrote to David, 'I got hold of old Tieck, and said "Now or never!" and he was amiable, and said "Now!"'

By 10 October he had composed an overture and a series of choral odes for sixteen male voices and orchestra. The play was staged at the Neues Palais in Potsdam on 28 October in front of a courtly Prussian audience which included Fanny Hensel, now once again his housemate. Mendelssohn's music for *Antigone*, Op. 55 is hardly remembered today, but at the time it was central to the spectacular success of this apparently abstruse venture. Berlioz, who called Frederick William IV 'the artists' King' partly on account of *Antigone*, regarded the revival as having 'brought the ancient world to life again', and the performance triggered an avalanche of productions throughout Germany and beyond, including several at Covent Garden in 1845.

For the remainder of 1841 Mendelssohn divided his time between Berlin and Leipzig, visiting the latter in November for a hectic round of concert-giving and private music-making during which he played to the Schumanns parts of the work conceived twelve years earlier among the ruins of Mary Queen of Scots' chapel at Holyrood and now once again at the forefront of his mind: the 'Scottish' Symphony. Mendelssohn's last symphony, and one of the undisputed masterpieces of his maturity, the 'Scottish' vies with the 'Italian' as the most performed of his symphonic works. The composer himself used the title only among friends – the work was published simply as his Symphony No. 3 in A minor, Op. 56 in 1843 – but Scottish elements are detectable throughout its four movements. The slow introduction reconvenes the shades of Mary's chapel, while the pentatonic theme of the ensuing scherzo – one of Mendelssohn's happiest inspirations – is infused with the spirit of Gaelic folk music. The last movement is perhaps the most successful of all his symphonic finales, a notable feature being the introduction in the coda of an entirely new, and again conspicuously Scottish, theme which brings the work to a rousing conclusion in an atmosphere redolent of communal celebration. Berlin may have released the symphony from its creative limbo, for it was there that Mendelssohn dated the finished score on 20 January 1842, but it was to Leipzig that he granted the first performance, which took place at the Gewandhaus under the composer's baton on 3 March.

By now the conductor of choice for festival committees throughout Germany, Mendelssohn co-directed the Lower Rhine Music Festival with Julius Rietz in Düsseldorf from 15 to 17 May, programming, among other works, Handel's *Israel in Egypt*, Beethoven's Fifth Symphony and his own *Lobgesang*. Twelve days later he and Cécile left the children with their maternal grandmother in Frankfurt and travelled to London together for the first time, staying south of the

Thames with Cécile's relatives the Beneckes in what was then the semi-rural seclusion of Denmark Hill. It was here that Mendelssohn wrote the most famous – not to say notorious – of his *Songs without Words*, the 'Spring Song' ('Frühlingslied'), later published as Op. 62 No. 6 with a dedication to Clara Schumann. Fresher, not least for being less familiar, are the eight piano miniatures Mendelssohn composed over three June days for the children of his host's family, six of which he published in 1846 as the *Children's Pieces* (*Kinderstücke*, also known as 'Christmas Pieces'), Op. 72, his final authorised opus. These little works capture something of the innocent wonder of childhood – musical testimony to a natural affinity with children demonstrated most delightfully by Mendelssohn's letters to his nephew Sebastian Hensel. A real-life coda to the *Kinderstücke* was provided several years later by the marriage of Mendelssohn's daughter Marie to one of the Benecke children, Victor.

p.138

The trip to England gave Cécile an opportunity to experience at first-hand her husband's phenomenal popularity in London society. The English premiere of the 'Scottish' Symphony at a Philharmonic concert on 13 June was a roaring success, and when Mendelssohn appeared at Exeter Hall four days later he was greeted even more tumultuously than he had been at the same venue five years earlier: an audience of some 3,000 people leapt to their feet, clapping and shouting, the applause being led by the prime minister, Sir Robert Peel. The highlights of the stay, however, were Mendelssohn's visits to Buckingham Palace, where he had a handwritten introduction to Prince Albert from Frederick William IV, the prince's cousin. Mendelssohn's first meeting with Victoria and Albert, then doting young twentysomethings in their second year of marriage, took place on 15 June. The queen's diary gives a fresh-minted account of the interview:

After dinner came Mendelssohn Bartholdy, whose acquaintance I was so anxious to make. Albert had already seen him the other morning. He is short, dark & Jewish looking, delicate, with a fine intellectual forehead. I should say he must be about 35 or 6. He is very pleasing & modest, & is greatly protected by the King of Prussia. He played first of all some of his 'Lieder ohne Worte' after which, his Serenade [Op. 43] & then, he asked us to give him a theme, upon which he could improvise. We gave him 2, 'Rule Britannia', & the Austrian National Anthem. He began immediately, & really I have never heard anything so beautiful; the way in which he blended them both together & changed over from one to the other, was quite wonderful as well as the exquisite harmony & feeling he puts into the variations, & the powerful rich chords, & modulations, which reminded one of all his beautiful compositions... We were all filled with the greatest admiration. Poor Mendelssohn was quite exhausted, when he had done playing.

If Victoria's record of her first meeting with the composer bears witness to the impressive musical literacy of the royal household, Mendelssohn's account of his second visit, on 9 July, gives a picture of its informality touchingly at odds with the starchily repressed image that has come down to us from Victoria's later years:

I found him [Albert] alone; and as we were talking away, the queen came in, also quite alone, in a house dress. She said she was obliged to leave for Claremont in an hour; 'But goodness! how it looks in here', she added, when she saw that the wind had littered the whole room, and even the pedals of the organ (which, by the way, made a very pretty feature

155

Mendelssohn playing to Queen Victoria and Prince Albert

of the room), with leaves of music from a large portfolio that
lay open. As she spoke, she knelt down and began picking up
the music; Prince Albert helped, and I too was not idle.

Mendelssohn sat down at the chamber organ to play the chorus 'How lovely are the messengers' from *St Paul*, and after a few bars the royal couple began to sing along, Albert at the same time expertly working the organ stops. This was the occasion, too, when Victoria sang Fanny's 'Italien' from Mendelssohn's first collection of songs, impressing him with her holding of the last high G which, he said, 'I have never heard better or purer or more natural from any amateur'. At the end of the evening, in an aristocratic exchange of mementos, the queen presented Mendelssohn with a ring engraved 'V.R., 1842' and granted him permission to dedicate the 'Scottish' Symphony to her in return.

By mid-July the Mendelssohns were back in Frankfurt for a brief reunion with their children before setting off to Switzerland for a holiday with Paul and Albertine. As they wound their way through Basel, Lausanne, Chamonix, Interlaken and Lucerne, Felix revelled in memories of previous visits and filled page after page of his sketchbooks with landscapes. 'I composed not even a bit of music,' he told Klingemann, 'but rather drew entire days, until my fingers and eyes ached.' He also indulged his passion for alpinism, one friend who joined them on a climbing expedition leaving a vivid pen-portrait of the composer as mountaineer: 'Always in front of everyone, Felix sprang like a chamois from rock to rock. His costume consisted of an Italian straw hat, black coat and breeches, white vest and collar. Apart from his hat and alpine shoes, he could have appeared straightaway at court.' From Interlaken Felix wrote to Lea, likening Switzerland to 'the best of books, which change along with you, showing a new side with each successive change', and fantasising about finding a Swiss country abode to which he and his family could escape for months at a time. 'Such at least are the daily thoughts and castles in the sky I build for myself', he added, wistfully.

The contrast with the chronic overcommitment of his real life must have seemed starker than ever when he returned from Switzerland at the beginning of September. Certainly when he returned to Berlin on 5 October (after taking part in a full round of music-making in Frankfurt, and conducting the first concert of the Gewandhaus season in Leipzig) Mendelssohn had every intention of extricating himself from what by now appeared an irredeemably false position in the king's service. What ensued, however, was a sort of farcical courtly dance. Over the next three weeks, Mendelssohn had two personal audiences with Frederick William, at which the monarch effectively closed his ears to his Kapellmeister's attempts to resign. Instead, he offered Mendelssohn the direction of a new, yet-to-be-founded cathedral choir and orchestra, the title General Music Director (Generalmusikdirektor) and the freedom to return to Leipzig until the new ensemble was up and running. With the exception of the last provision, it is hard to see what in these nebulous new arrangements could overcome Mendelssohn's reluctance to stay bound to the Prussian court, especially since the king's previous plans for a new foundation – the conservatoire Mendelssohn was meant to be heading – had not progressed beyond the drawing board for the last fifteen months. But overcome it they did, no doubt with a little help from Lea, who had been devastated at the prospect of her son leaving Berlin again when he had broken his intentions to her the evening before his second audience.

Another royal audience awaited him back in Saxony, this time with King Frederick Augustus II in Dresden. Here Mendelssohn was more successful in keeping to his own agenda: he emerged having relinquished the Saxon Kapellmeistership (which he felt was incompatible with his new position at the Prussian court) and having rallied the king's support for a new music conservatoire in Leipzig by persuading him to hypothecate to its foundation a 20,000-thaler bequest from the will of a prominent lawyer. In contrast to the slow-grinding mills of Prussian bureaucracy, Mendelssohn had already assembled a virtual faculty by December, and the conservatoire opened its doors to students at the beginning of April. Schumann, the Thomaskantor Moritz Hauptmann and Ferdinand David were among its teaching staff. Moscheles was also successfully persuaded to join in due course. Mendelssohn himself, though by no means a natural in the classroom, would teach piano, ensemble and composition at the new institution, of which he was characteristically keen not to be regarded as the director.

Mendelssohn's grateful resumption of his Leipzig life in the closing months of 1842 was interrupted on 12 December by the sudden death of his mother in Berlin. Lea's passing marked the end of an era in the close-knit life of the Mendelssohn clan. 'The point of union is now gone...' Felix wrote to Paul. 'We are children no longer.' But it also severed one of his strongest emotional bonds with the city of his childhood. 'What made me specially cling to Berlin... no longer exists,' he wrote to Hiller on 19 January 1843. The very same day he composed the grief-stricken 'Song without Words' in E minor, collected the following year as Op. 62 No. 3 and now generally known as the 'Funeral March' ('Trauermarsch').

As after Abraham's death seven years earlier, Mendelssohn coped with his loss by immersing himself in work, revising his 1834 concert aria *Infelice* and *Die erste Walpurgisnacht*. In late January he was rehearsing the new version of the latter for its Gewandhaus premiere on 2 February when Berlioz walked into the hall, having just arrived in Leipzig on his first German concert tour. Berlioz was enraptured by the 'whirling momentum and sweep' of the music and, when Mendelssohn stepped down from the rostrum, theatrically requested the master's baton in exchange for his own – 'trading brass for gold', as he put it. The Frenchman's 'heavy oak cudgel' arrived the next day with an extravagant note *à la* James Fenimore Cooper – a sample of the 'odd manners' Fanny Hensel said rubbed people up the wrong way throughout Berlioz's Leipzig visit:

> *To Chief Mendelssohn!*
> *Great chief! We promised to exchange our tomahawks; here's mine! It is rough, yours is simple. Only squaws and palefaces like ornamented weapons. Be my brother! and when the great Spirit has sent us hunting in the land of souls, may our warriors hang our tomahawks together over the door of the meeting-house.*

Despite his personal reservations about his friend's music, Mendelssohn had agreed to mount two all-Berlioz concerts at the Gewandhaus. The centrepiece of the first one, the *Symphonie fantastique*, provoked intense controversy in Leipzig, but Berlioz was delighted with the orchestra's account of the work (even if Mendelssohn had to step in to play the second movement's harp passages on the piano when the harpist messed them up!).

If Mendelssohn's relations with Berlioz represent one of music history's happier essays in the negotiation of aesthetic differences, another of his encounters in these months represents one of its most invidious. On 7 June Mendelssohn travelled to Dresden to attend the unveiling of a statue of King Frederick Augustus I, for which he had composed a cantata for male voices and brass on the Saxon national anthem *Gott segne Sachsenland* ('God Bless Saxony', sung to the same tune as that of *God Save the Queen*). The work was conducted not by Mendelssohn himself but by the recently appointed Dresden Kapellmeister: an ambitious thirty-year-old named Richard Wagner.

Mendelssohn's path had already crossed with Wagner's on a few occasions, most recently in April when Mendelssohn conducted *St Paul* in Dresden. Wagner had described the effect of hearing the oratorio under the composer's baton in revelatory terms – 'Mendelssohn Bartholdy showed us, in all perfection, a work which is a testimony to the highest flowering of art' – and after meeting Mendelssohn again in June he wrote him a fulsome letter ending, 'I am proud to belong to the nation which produced you and your *St Paul*.' It would not be long, however, before the nationalism of the sentiment displaced the admiration. In his notorious essay *On Judaism in Music* (*Über das Judentum in der Musik*), published pseudonymously three years after Mendelssohn's death, Wagner made critically respectable the toxic mixture of aesthetics and anti-Semitism that would fester in German culture for decades before hardening into policy under the Nazis. Just seven years after their meeting in Dresden, Mendelssohn, far from being an exemplar of all that was most admirable in German music, had become, by Wagner's lights, a composer permanently excluded from true greatness by virtue of his Jewish roots.

Whatever the psychological dynamics of this *volte face*, in retrospect one can plot a growing sense of rivalry through Wagner's relations with Mendelssohn in the 1840s.

In November 1842 Wagner had shown an almost paranoid defensiveness when Mendelssohn overheard him playing the Venusberg theme from his work-in-progress *Tannhäuser* and innocently asked him what it was; and even while writing to Mendelssohn his gushing letter after the statue-unveiling, Wagner was telling his half-sister that everyone agreed his own contribution to the celebrations, an *a cappella* male part-song 'which was straightforward and uplifting, knocked Mendelssohn's over-elaborate and artificial composition into a cocked hat'. Similarly, Wagner did not hesitate to attribute to Mendelssohn the failure of his *Tannhäuser* Overture at the Gewandhaus in February 1846, Mendelssohn's one and only foray into Wagner conducting. The history of the arts affords all too many instances of personal and political animus fuelling aesthetic rivalries, but there are few parallels for the ugly line of historical causation that runs directly from Wagner's *Über das Judentum* in 1850 to Mendelssohn's extirpation from the German canon by Hitler's aesthetic commissars in the 1930s.

The summer of 1843 was a productive one for Mendelssohn. He compiled for publication his Six Songs (*Sechs Lieder*), Op. 57, the earliest of which date from 1839, including the second song 'Hirtenlied', subsequently arranged as a part-song and posthumously published as Op. 88 No. 3. He also saw into print his third volume of part-songs for mixed voices, Op. 59 (confusingly another *Sechs Lieder*), most of which had been composed during the previous few months. More substantial than these offerings is the four-movement Cello Sonata No. 2 in D major, Op. 58, written for his brother Paul. Here a joyfully full-bodied opening subject sets the tone for one of Mendelssohn's most extroverted first movements. The ensuing *Allegretto scherzando*, with its mischievous pizzicato effects, is more impish than elfin, and the experimental slow movement interposes a heartfelt dialogue of arpeggiated chorale and recitative before the finale returns us to the ebullient world of the opening movement.

Shortly after completing the Cello Sonata Mendelssohn composed a Capriccio in E minor – effectively a prelude and fugue – for string quartet, dated 5 July and posthumously published as Op. 81 No. 3. Nine days later he was commanded by Frederick William IV to produce an arrangement of the Lutheran Te Deum *Herr Gott dich loben wir* for the forthcoming celebrations of the millennium of the German Reich. He fulfilled the commission in just two days, producing a setting for two four-part choirs, trombones, strings and organ which he conducted in the cathedral in Berlin amid much commemorative ceremony on 6 August.

Mendelssohn hardly needed the latter command to remind him of his ties to the Prussian court. The new cathedral choir and orchestra began to function in May, prompting yet more renegotiation of his exact terms of engagement, much shuttling to and fro on the Leipzig–Berlin line, and a great deal of irritation. In the meantime, he continued working on the incidental music for three further theatrical collaborations with Tieck. To compound Felix's frustration, changes in the king's travel timetable postponed the scheduled premieres of the first two projects: Sophocles' *Oedipus at Colonos* and Jean Racine's *Athalie*. The third premiere took place as planned on 14 October 1843. The play was Shakespeare's *A Midsummer Night's Dream*.

Mendelssohn's incidental music to *A Midsummer Night's Dream*, Op. 61, is not only one of his greatest works but also one of the most remarkable undertakings in musical history. In adding thirteen numbers to the overture he had composed as a seventeen-year-old in 1826, Mendelssohn recreated with a magic worthy of the play itself a world he had last visited half a lifetime ago. The new music takes

website

ideas from the overture (the four wind chords, the fairy music, Bottom's braying) and weaves them into a seamless fabric that perfectly recaptures the spirit of the original. Frequently performed as stand-alone concert items, the four instrumental entr'actes or intermezzos are the most familiar numbers today. These include the Scherzo (No. 1) which neatly conjures the ambiguous nature of the spirit Puck,

CD 2 [7]

and the sublime 'Notturno' (No. 7). But the melodramas which accompany stretches of the action also contain some of Mendelssohn's finest music, including in No. 4 the eerie chromaticism of the strings that accompany Oberon's and Puck's casting of the spells, and in No. 10 a 'Funeral March' for the death of Pyramus which uncannily prefigures Mahler's parodic use of the form in his First Symphony. The best-known number of all is the entr'acte between Acts 4 and 5, in which Mendelssohn gave the world a piece of music that can perhaps lay claim to having more personal significance for more people than any other: the 'Wedding March' (No. 9). So overexposed has it become, indeed, that it is impossible to hear it afresh even in its original context, where it prepares the ground for the multiple weddings of the play's final act. As the critic Donald Tovey wrote: 'Neither the greatest music nor the greatest poetry in the world was ever meant to stand the strain that custom has put upon *The* Wedding March.' The finale, one of two vocal numbers in the work, begins and ends with the four timeless chords which frame the overture, closing one of the most bewitching creative circles in all music.

The premiere was not without its problems. Unbeknown to Mendelssohn, Tieck had recast the five acts of Schlegel's translation into three, which resulted in two of the intermezzos being performed with the curtain up, including the 'Notturno', for the duration of which the audience were left to consider the less than dramatic spectacle of the lovers sleeping on stage. Furthermore, the fact that the play was effectively the royal equivalent of corporate entertainment meant that there was a long hiatus in the middle while refreshments were noisily served to the courtiers in the front rows. Despite such infelicities, however, the production transferred successfully to the public stage at the Berlin Schauspielhaus, where it brought the house down.

In creating the new cathedral choir and orchestra, Frederick William had kept his side of the bargain struck with Mendelssohn at their audience the previous autumn, no matter how resistant to contractual codification his plans might be in the hands of his ministers. After commuting to Leipzig to conduct several concerts at the beginning of the Gewandhaus season, therefore, Mendelssohn moved back to Berlin on 25 November with his whole family (now augmented by the birth in May of his fourth child, Felix August Eduard, a sickly boy who would die before his eighth birthday). Over the next four weeks he fulfilled another clause of his new contract by directing a series of orchestral soirées at the Singakademie, and in December he conducted the cathedral choir for the first time in his new role as director of sacred music.

Mendelssohn's appointment to this directorship took place against the background of royal reforms to the liturgy, designed to help fuse the central denominational rift in German Protestantism between the Calvinist (Reformed) and Lutheran traditions. The controversy aroused by the musical implications of the new liturgy – what kind of music should accompany services and at what junctures – seems remote and arcane today, and even at the time was felt by many, including Mendelssohn himself, to shed more heat than light. From the perspective of musical history, though, its most important outcome was the fund of sacred works

165

Mendelssohn composed between December 1843 and March 1844 for the Christmas, New Year, Passion Sunday and Good Friday services at the cathedral in Berlin. These divide into a series of psalm settings, designed as introits to the services, and several short *a cappella* settings, intended to be sung before the Alleluia. The former include Psalm 2 (for double chorus and organ, posthumously published in *a cappella* form as Op. 78 No. 1), Psalm 98 (for solo voices, double choir, orchestra and organ, Op. 91) and *a cappella* settings of Psalms 43 and 22 (Op. 78 Nos 2 & 3). Also composed for the cathedral choir was a setting of Psalm 100 for unaccompanied chorus, once believed to have been intended for the New Israelite Temple in Hamburg, by whom Mendelssohn was indeed commissioned to compose some psalms at this time. Four of the *a cappella* settings sung before the Alleluia were among the fine pieces published after Mendelssohn's death as the *Sechs Sprüche* ('Six Proverbs'), Op. 79, which include in the rapt New Year, Passion Sunday and Good Friday settings 'Herr Gott, du bist unsre Zuflucht' ('Dear God, you are our refuge', No. 2), 'Herr, gedenke nicht unser Übelthaten' ('Lord, remember not our wrongdoings', No. 4) and 'Um unsrer Sünden' ('For the sake of our sins', No. 6), three perfect gems of Mendelssohn's sacred writing.

Far the best-known religious work of his time as director of sacred music, however, was not written for Berlin at all. Rather, his setting of William Bartholomew's paraphrase of Psalm 55, *Hear My Prayer* for soprano, choir and organ, was composed in January 1844 for a series of sacred concerts held in London, where it received its first performance a year later. It quickly established itself as a fixture in the English cathedral repertoire, its final section 'O for the wings of a dove' attaining the status of a favourite parlour-piece in the Victorian and Edwardian period.

Mendelssohn's dealings with the clerical hierarchy in Berlin proved no less fraught than his relations with the secular authorities. In particular, his use of orchestral accompaniments in the Christmas and New Year settings, and especially of the supposedly profane harp in Psalm 98, was criticised as contrary to the purified spirit of the revised liturgy, and even before directing the Easter services in 1844 he was seeking to shed his composing commitments to the cathedral. Not long afterwards he crossed swords once again with the king's ministers, who interpreted as downright refusal his lukewarm response to a royal request to compose incidental music for Aeschylus' *Eumenides*. This altercation led to a forthright exchange of letters between Bunsen and Mendelssohn, who informed the minister that while he wanted to conform to the king's wishes, 'if I cannot do it with a *good artistic conscience*, then I shall try honestly to express… my objections, and if I do not make my point then I must go'. As soon as the concert season ended he left Berlin for Leipzig and Frankfurt. By 8 May he was in London, where he had been invited to conduct a series of Philharmonic concerts by his friend, the young English composer William Sterndale Bennett, some of whose works he had premiered at the Gewandhaus.

As always, London provided relief from the frustrations of German musical life. 'My stay in England was wonderful,' he wrote to his brother Paul shortly after returning to Germany; 'I have never been received anywhere with such universal kindness as I was this time, and played more music in the two months than I usually do in two years'. Certainly, the pace of his public and private concert-giving would alone have exhausted a less resilient man. At the Philharmonic concerts he introduced to the English public both his 'Scottish' Symphony and a young violin prodigy whom he had taken under his wing in Leipzig. This was the thirteen-year-old Joseph Joachim, later to rank among the most celebrated violinists of the second half of the nineteenth century. In deference to Mendelssohn, the Philharmonic Society waived its no-prodigies rule to relish Joachim's precocious account of Beethoven's Violin Concerto. Less successful was Mendelssohn's attempt to introduce Schubert's 'Great' C major Symphony to a London audience. The musicians could not stomach the repeated triplets in the finale and he angrily withdrew the work from rehearsal, substituting the Overture to Schubert's opera *Fierrabras*, which was duly savaged by the critics. Meanwhile, Mendelssohn's social life was as unremitting as his musical activity. Among his myriad engagements, which generally kept him up until the early hours of the morning, he had audiences with Victoria and Albert, to whom he presented an arrangement for piano duet of seven of his *Songs without Words*, including the newly published Op. 62 collection. He also dined with Charles Dickens, whose *Pickwick Papers* he had been reading avidly back home. Somehow he even found time to complete for publication his Six Vocal Duets (*Sechs zweistimmige Lieder*), Op. 63 and to edit Handel's *Israel in Egypt* for the Handel Society – an early, and at the time controversial, exercise in strict adherence to the composer's original intentions.

On returning to Germany, he allowed himself a rare interlude of relaxation. On 13 July he joined the rest of his family at Soden near Frankfurt, where he revelled in the country air, the exuberance of the children and, above all, the lack of pressing engagements. Even here, however, he was scarcely idle. At the end of the month he travelled to Zweibrücken to conduct *St Paul* and *Die erste Walpurgisnacht* at the Palatinate Music Festival (and did full justice to the local wines!). He began to edit Bach's organ works for the English publisher Charles Coventry, for whom he also started writing the series of organ pieces that would reach their final form the following year as the Six Organ Sonatas, Op. 65. And in August he composed an *a cappella* motet on words from Psalm 91, *Denn er hat seinen Engeln befohlen über dir* ('For he shall give his angels charge over thee'), in reaction to news of a failed assassination attempt on Frederick William IV – a reminder of the political turbulence that would explode, the year after Mendelssohn's death, in the revolutions of 1848. (The setting later found a permanent home in *Elijah*.)

It is also to these idyllic summer weeks in Soden that we owe one of the greatest of all Mendelssohn's compositions, the Violin Concerto in E minor, Op. 64. Like so many of his

masterpieces, this concerto had been forming in his mind for several years; the unforgettable opening idea had occurred to him as long ago as the summer of 1838. We do not know what led Mendelssohn to take it up again in 1844, but by mid-September he had finished a manuscript of the work and was discussing details with its dedicatee, his old friend and Leipzig colleague Ferdinand David.

Ferdinand David, dedicatee of Mendelssohn's Violin Concerto in E minor

The Violin Concerto is one of those rare works that remain entirely fresh despite their ubiquity. The opening subject of the first movement is among the most haunting themes ever written, and its return in the recapitulation, emerging from behind the filigree of the soloist's hushed arpeggios, is one of the most magical moments in all music. As in the two mature piano concertos, the three movements are connected, both thematically

and by transitional passages. The slow movement has the qualities of a cavatina, with the soloist carrying the thematic material throughout, while the finale has something of the same playful exuberance as the music for *A Midsummer Night's Dream*. Long ranked with the violin concertos of Beethoven, Brahms and Tchaikovsky as one of the greatest works of its kind, Mendelssohn's Op. 64 nonetheless remains *sui generis*. As the Mendelssohn scholar Thomas Grey has insightfully remarked, 'more than any other of Mendelssohn's works (the "Wedding March" excepted), it seems almost to have dissociated itself from its composer and to lead an autonomous existence, like some product of nature'. The concerto was premiered by David in Leipzig on 13 March 1845 under the baton of Mendelssohn's protégé and friend, the young Danish composer Niels Gade (whose own First Symphony Mendelssohn had premiered at the Gewandhaus two years earlier).

Writing to Baron von Bunsen in the aftermath of the *Eumenides* debacle in May, Mendelssohn had warned the minister that he could not remain in Berlin 'under such unstable conditions'. At the end of September, fortified by his London experiences and his productive holiday in Soden, he returned to the Prussian capital determined to resign from the king's service once and for all. This time Frederick William made only a token effort to dissuade him. In an audience early in October the king bowed to the inevitable and released the composer from his duties and residency in Berlin, though Mendelssohn agreed to make himself available for occasional royal commissions and festivals in exchange for a handsome retainer of 1,000 thalers. He remained in the Prussian capital for the rest of the autumn, conducting his last two orchestral soirées and a command performance of *St Paul* at the Singakademie. Then on 30 November 1844, after bidding farewell to his sister Fanny, he shook the dust of the city from his feet. 'The first step out of Berlin is the first step towards happiness,' he wrote to Eduard Devrient. He had less than three years left in which to enjoy his freedom.

Chapter 7

The Final Years
(1845–1847)

The Final Years (1845–1847)

As 1844 drew to a close Mendelssohn was, as one of the many visitors who beat a path to his door observed, 'in the noon of his fame'. Widely regarded as the world's greatest living composer, he was also a deeply troubled man, torn between the conflicting demands of public, private and creative life. It was a conflict by now rapidly sapping the energy and resilience that had sustained him throughout his whirlwind of a career. The desire to step out of the 'eternal mad rush', to devote himself to his family and to composition, had been a theme in Mendelssohn's letters since at least the early months of his marriage. In his last years it becomes a yearning leitmotif. As he wrote to his sister Rebecka in January 1845:

> I have for some time felt the necessity for complete rest – not travelling, not conducting, not performing – so keenly that I am compelled to yield to it, and hope to be able to order my life accordingly for the whole year for repose.

For a while, at least, his hope seemed realistic. He settled himself with Cécile and the children in Frankfurt, waxing lyrical to his brother Paul about the joys of fatherhood and of long walks in the spring countryside. He resisted Frederick Augustus II's attempts to lure him back into employment in Saxony, and requests from Frederick William IV to head a new school of composition in Berlin and to compose music for Aeschylus' *Oresteia*. He even turned down an invitation from the recently formed New York Philharmonic Society to direct a grand music festival in the United States, a venture, he wrote to the Society's president, 'which I would have been most happy to undertake some 3 or 4 years ago' but which was now 'beyond my reach'.

Above all, he devoted himself to composition, that 'inward work', as he described it to a Frankfurt friend, which his performing and administrative life had for so many years forced to the sidelines. A projected symphony in C major remained in fragmentary draft, but on 2 April he completed the Six Organ Sonatas, Op. 65, which he had begun the previous year in nearby Soden. The pieces had evolved a long way from the set of 'voluntaries' specified in the original English commission. In their final form, the sonatas have been credited with consolidating the Bachian tradition of organ music that Mendelssohn had played a key part in reviving with his Preludes and Fugues, Op. 37, and of which he was by common consent the greatest exponent of his time. A cornerstone of the organ repertoire, the Organ Sonatas are not actually sonatas in the Classical sense at all. Rather, they are relatively loose agglomerations of individual movements, in which fugal and chorale elements feature prominently. Nos 1, 2 and 5 have three movements each, Nos 4 and 6 four, and No. 3 only two (the second being little more than a lyrical pendant to the imposing fugue of the first). The heterogeneity of the sonatas' origins is not limited to the nature of the commission. At least two of the movements incorporate material written years before: the introduction to the first movement of No. 3, for example, is probably the processional intended for Fanny's wedding in 1829. Mendelssohn set great store by these organ sonatas, which he saw in part as

CD 2 9

website

an instruction manual for the instrument, and he arranged for them to be published simultaneously in London, Leipzig, Paris and Milan.

At the end of April he finished another major work, the Piano Trio No. 2 in C minor, Op. 66. Dedicated to Louis Spohr, this work has never quite matched the First Piano Trio in popularity, though it has been regarded by some critics as an even finer work. The third-movement scherzo is a reminder of how recently Mendelssohn had revisited the gossamer world of *A Midsummer Night's Dream*. The trio's most striking moment, however, comes in the finale, where Mendelssohn introduces a chorale subject at once unexpected and yet wholly natural, and in the final pages creates from it one of his most uplifting fusions of secular and sacred song. Another large-scale chamber work that has remained in the shadow of its more immediately accessible predecessor was finished less than ten weeks later. This was the String Quintet No. 2 in B flat major, completed on 8 July and nowadays heard less often than the youthful String Quintet in A major. Mendelssohn, who was unconvinced by the finale, withheld it from publication, and it appeared only after his death as Op. 87.

Between these two compositions Mendelssohn completed the compilation of his *Songs without Words*, Op. 67, the sixth and one of the most characterful of his collections. Two of the songs have acquired familiar titles: the fourth, a teeming *perpetuum mobile*, has long been known as the 'Spinning song' ('Spinnerlied'), and the sixth as 'Berceuse' ('Wiegenlied'), though it seems on the face of it to belong as much to the ballroom as to the nursery. The collection was dedicated to Sophie Rosen, the younger sister of Mendelssohn's old friend Friedrich; to Felix's delight she was now the fiancée of Karl Klingemann, in whose arms her brother had died in London in 1837. Two further sets of *Songs without Words*, Opp. 85 and 102, including some pieces Mendelssohn considered for inclusion in Op. 67, were published after his death, but the Op. 67 set is the last that the composer himself approved for publication.

Gradually, though, and with seeming inevitability, the pull of institutional musical life re-exerted itself. Around the same time that Mendelssohn finished the String Quintet No. 2, Frederick William notified him that *Oedipus at Colonos*, for which he had completed his incidental music in February, would be staged in the autumn. And when Frederick Augustus made further overtures to him, Mendelssohn agreed also to resume his teaching work at the Leipzig Conservatoire and his direction of the Gewandhaus (though now in tandem with Niels Gade). By the end of the summer of 1845, therefore, Mendelssohn had once more allowed himself to be drawn into the service of two different courts – precisely the arrangement that had proved so debilitatingly untenable over the preceding three years. The familiar pattern was soon re-established. Between mid-August and the beginning of October, he found himself shuttling backwards and forwards between Saxony and Prussia. He set up house with his family in a roomy apartment in 3 Königstrasse, which would be their permanent Leipzig home for the remainder of his life; the Mendelssohns' last child, Fanny Henriette Elisabeth (Lili) was born there on 19 September within days of their moving in. He discussed *Oedipus at Colonos* with Tieck in Berlin and his Saxon contract with the court in Dresden, and on 5 October took to the rostrum once more for the first concert of the new season at the Gewandhaus, where he was greeted like a returning hero. He dived back into the daily routines of the Conservatoire, too, drawing up

Mendelssohn's
last residence:
3 Königstrasse,
Leipzig

meticulous reports on the students' work. It is as if, schooled from childhood to be always active, he had to make up in commitment of time any deficit in enthusiasm for the task in hand. That he no longer felt such enthusiasm is evident from everything we know of his life during this period. Friends noted how he had aged, and how short-tempered he had become. Indeed, his jadedness leached the colour even from his past achievements as a musical executive. Writing to a friend in Frankfurt, he looked forward to the time when he could return to domestic seclusion in the area, claiming: 'I have followed all my external musical pursuits, such as conducting, etc., purely from a sense of duty, never from inclination...'

For the present, though, domestic seclusion was as much a pipe dream as his hopes for retirement to Switzerland had been in 1842. There was hardly a gap in his schedule. On

1 November 1845 he directed the premiere of *Oedipus at Colonos* in the Neues Palais in Potsdam, but neither it nor the public performance at the Schauspielhaus nine days later aroused the enthusiasm generated by his previous Sophoclean excursion, *Antigone*. More successful was the first performance of *Athalie* at the Charlottenburg Palace in Berlin on 1 December. Queen Victoria requested a copy of the work, which was given its English premiere at Windsor Castle a month later, and the entr'acte 'War March of the Priests' – to judge by the music, a distinctly unbelligerent clerisy – attained during the nineteenth century a popular status similar to that of the 'Wedding March'. (Indeed, it was enough of a standard in the 1870s for Thomas Hardy to cite it as a musical correlative for Eustacia Vye's character in *The Return of the Native*.)

Three days after the Berlin premiere of *Athalie* a young Scandinavian soprano made her memorable Leipzig debut. Jenny Lind, the 'Swedish Nightingale', was then twenty-five years old and already established on the operatic A-list for her purity of tone and her (much promoted) simplicity of manner. She had already captivated Berlin – and Mendelssohn – with her performances in *Norma*, *Don Giovanni* and *Der Freischütz*, and her appearance at the Gewandhaus confirmed her as a performer of phenomenal popular appeal. The attachment that developed between her and Mendelssohn was (to the discomfiture of Cécile) the subject of much comment and speculation during the composer's lifetime, as it has continued to be for biographers since. Mendelssohn sent her songs of a romantic bent and wrote to her that she was always in his thoughts, while Lind would later claim that Mendelssohn was 'the only person who brought fulfilment to my spirit'. They seem to have spent as much time as possible in each other's company, and at the end of May 1846 cruised down the Rhine together (albeit with a chaperone) to the Lower Rhine Music Festival in Aachen, where Mendelssohn conducted her in Haydn's *Creation* and other works. According to his friend Hans Christian Andersen (himself so smitten by Lind that he mythologised her voice in his fairytale *The Nightingale*), the composer did everything he could to advance Lind's career, proclaiming, 'There will not be born, in a whole century, another being so gifted as she'.

However far Mendelssohn's feelings went beyond aesthetic infatuation, Lind certainly inspired him to think about opera again: 'if I do not attain to the composition of a fairly good opera now, and for you,' he wrote to her, 'I shall never accomplish it at all'. He discussed with the poet Emanuel Geibel a libretto based on the Rhine legend of the Lorelei, and revisited the idea of *The Tempest*, this time with the French playwright Eugène Scribe. But his words to Lind would prove prophetic. *The Tempest* went the same way as Mendelssohn's previous collaboration on the subject with Immermann (the London promoter who had hopefully advertised it before a note was written had to replace it with *I masnadieri* by the thirty-four-year-old Verdi), and the music for *Die Lorelei* remained a tantalising fragment at Mendelssohn's death.

A more lasting memorial to Lind's voice, however, was the central work of Mendelssohn's final years, the oratorio *Elijah*, Op. 70, the soprano part of which was written specifically for her. The composer's plans for the work had lain dormant for years when an invitation from the Birmingham Musical Festival for 1846 gave them a kick-start and led him to pick up libretto discussions with Schubring where he had left off in 1839. Schubring sprang into action, quickly drafting a text for the first part of the oratorio. The music still had to compete for time with Mendelssohn's other commitments. In addition to his Gewandhaus concert-giving and his direction of the Aachen Music Festival, in mid-June he took part in a rambunctious German-Flemish Choral Festival at Cologne, where he premiered his setting of Schiller's *An die Künstler* ('To Artists') for male chorus and brass band, Op. 68. And a few days earlier, at the 600th anniversary of the feast of Corpus Christi in Liège, he had attended the premiere of one of his most significant sacred works, a setting for solo voices, chorus and orchestra of Thomas Aquinas's *Lauda Sion*, Op. 73, the last and perhaps the weightiest of Mendelssohn's Catholic settings.

The 'Swedish Nightingale': Jenny Lind

Despite such engagements, however, throughout the first seven months of 1846 Mendelssohn was able to focus his creative efforts on *Elijah* with a single-mindedness almost unparalleled in his later years. The first version of the score was completed on 11 August, less than a fortnight before the Birmingham Festival was due to begin. A week later he was in London, rehearsing with the orchestra and soloists. Jenny Lind had, unfortunately, decided that opera was a better medium than oratorio in which to make her English debut, so the part Mendelssohn had imagined for her was sung by the temperamental soprano Maria Caradori-Allan. (When the latter asked for one number to be transposed down a tone, the composer refused on the forthright grounds that she was more dispensable than the original key!) On 23 August he took the train to Birmingham with the musicians and on the morning of 26 August *Elijah* received its world premiere in the Town Hall before an audience of 2,000. 'Never before has a piece of mine gone so splendidly at the first performance, and been received so enthusiastically by the musicians and the listeners,' Mendelssohn reported to his brother Paul. To judge by other reports of the occasion, this was a considerable understatement. The audience threw restraint to the winds. 'Mendelssohn's triumph at yesterday's performance was something quite incredible, unheard of,' Moscheles wrote to his wife the following day, while *The Times*, describing Mendelssohn unequivocally as 'the greatest composer of the age', reported:

> *The last note of* Elijah *was drowned in a long-continued unanimous volley of plaudits, vociferous and deafening. It was as though enthusiasm, long checked, had suddenly burst its bonds and filled the air with shouts of exultation. Mendelssohn, evidently overpowered, bowed his acknowledgment, and quickly descended from his position in the conductor's rostrum; but he was compelled to appear again, amidst renewed cheers and huzzas. Never was there a more complete triumph – never a more thorough and speedy recognition of a great work of art.*

Near-universally regarded by contemporaries as the apogee of Mendelssohn's achievement as a composer, *Elijah* has suffered a similar, though less precipitate, decline to that of *St Paul*. It was a perennial of choral societies throughout the nineteenth century, second only to Handel's *Messiah* in popularity. But, designed as it was to appeal to English taste – William Bartholomew had adapted the libretto to the cadences of the King James Authorised Version of the Bible – its association with Victorianism did it no favours in the revolution of sensibilities around the turn of the century, and it was a prime target of George Bernard Shaw, who famously inveighed against Mendelssohn's 'despicable oratorio mongering'. Even today, when Shaw, Lytton Strachey and like-minded critics have themselves become part of the history of taste, it is hard to recover the impact of those early performances. *Elijah* is a far more sustained and powerful work than *St Paul*, but some of the solo numbers – Obadiah's 'If with all your hearts' (No. 4), for example, or the angel's 'O rest in the Lord' (No. 31) – seem fatally weakened by their association with the more unctuous strain in Victorian piety. To modern ears, too, such climactic numbers as the final chorus of Part 1 can speak as much of self-satisfaction as of worship.

A series of episodes from the life of the Old Testament prophet, *Elijah*, like its predecessor, falls into two parts. The action now, however, is advanced not by a narrator but by the principals themselves, with the chorus taking on different mantles (as, for example, the worshippers of Baal and the Israelites) as well as commentating on the unfolding events. Part 1 begins magisterially *in medias res* with Elijah's recitative prophesying that God will curse the faithless Israelites with seven years of drought. Only afterwards does Mendelssohn give us the overture, the darkly troubled music of which invokes the people's sufferings. The dramatic core of Part 1 is Elijah's confrontation with the adherents of Baal – close relatives, it seems, of the heathens of *Die erste Walpurgisnacht*, even if the latter's frenetic choruses make the Baalites' invocations to their god sound curiously underpowered. In contrast with *St Paul*, there is little slackening of the dramatic drive in Part 2, which culminates in Elijah's encounter with the Lord – where the chorus takes on the role of the seraphim in one of the work's most breathtakingly beautiful episodes (No. 35)

Elijah did not foretell how long the drought would continue, but in Luke Ch 4 v 25 we read that it lasted three years and six months.

183

– and his final ascent to heaven. The emotional crux of this part, however, is the prophet's aria 'It is enough' (No. 26), in which many commentators have heard an autobiographical cry of terminal world-weariness. It is here above all, perhaps, that one can see in *Elijah* a surrogate for the mature opera Mendelssohn was never to write.

Even as he walked around Birmingham on the afternoon of the premiere, Mendelssohn began revising *Elijah*, and much of the rest of 1846 was devoted to the task. Only four new compositions interrupted the work between 6 September, when he left England, and the end of the year. For the pastor who had officiated at his wedding, he wrote a setting of the Huguenot poem *Venez et chantez les louanges de ce Christ* ('Come and Sing the Praises of this Christ'), a *cantique* not published in complete form until 1997. And for the cathedral choir in Berlin he composed two new *Sprüche* (completing the set of six that were published shortly after his death as Op. 79) and a ten-movement setting for *a cappella* eight-voice choir of the *Deutsche Liturgie* ('German Liturgy'), which had to wait a year longer than the *cantique* to be published in full.

Meanwhile, there was no reduction in the pace of his public life, either at the Conservatoire or at the Gewandhaus. The new Gewandhaus season – the last he would see through to the end – began on 4 October, and was not without controversy. On 5 November Mendelssohn's premiere of Schumann's Symphony No. 2 in C major, Op. 61 stirred up the reservoir of anti-Semitism that was seldom far below the surface of German cultural life. The symphony's poor reception was somehow blamed on Mendelssohn's preparedness to encore another piece on the programme, the Overture to Rossini's *William Tell*, which one Leipzig journal interpreted, bizarrely, as a 'Mosaic' conspiracy. Mendelssohn was prevailed upon to repeat the symphony at a concert a few days later, but the incident damaged relations with Schumann, who was already showing signs of the mental instability that would institutionalise him in the final years of his life. By the end of 1846 Mendelssohn, further shaken by the death of his long-standing servant and friend Johann Krebs, was once again fantasising about shelving all his public commitments to concentrate on composition and domestic music-making. But, as ever, he seemed unable to step off the carousel. Only days before writing to his brother Paul in October that he now saw it as his duty to give up the professional office he had once seen it as his duty to fill, he had accepted an invitation from the Sacred Harmonic Society in London to premiere the revised *Elijah* in April 1847.

Spurred on by this self-imposed deadline, Mendelssohn continued his work on Part 1 of the oratorio through the final months of the year, and in mid-December played parts of the score to Fanny in Berlin; it was the last time he would see his sister. The early months of the New Year, too, were taken up with revisions and preparation of the work for publication. Moscheles was among those who found incomprehensible Mendelssohn's obsessive reworking of a score already hailed by *The Times* as 'one of the most extraordinary achievements of human intelligence'. But in the final analysis the only estimation that mattered to Mendelssohn was his own. As he had written to Klingemann in December, he was determined 'not to rest until such a work is as good as I can possibly make it – even though most people know little and care less about these things'.

On 2 April 1847 Mendelssohn gave what would be his last public performance in Leipzig, conducting *St Paul* at the Paulinerkirche, and six days later left for his tenth and final visit to England. One of his former pupils at the Leipzig

Conservatoire, the composer and pianist William Smith Rockstro, was shocked to see how he had aged in the last year or so. Two months earlier Mendelssohn had celebrated his thirty-eighth birthday, but his appearance and bearing were those of a much older man. The years of ceaseless overactivity were fast catching up with him, and he had, said Rockstro, a 'worn look, quite foreign to his usual expression – a look of pain'. Despite his exhaustion, however, Mendelssohn conducted no fewer than six performances of *Elijah* in the space of two weeks, in London, Manchester and Birmingham. Queen Victoria and Prince Albert were in the audience for the second performance at Exeter Hall on 23 April, Albert helping bind Mendelssohn's fortunes still more tightly to those of the Victorian age with a much-publicised tribute beginning: 'To the noble artist who, surrounded by the Baal-worship of false art, through genius and study has been able, like a second Elijah, to remain true to the service of true art...' The royal family were at the head of Mendelssohn's hectic visiting schedule, too. On 1 May he spent an hour with Victoria and Albert at Buckingham Palace, playing, as the queen noted in her diary,

> *some new compositions, with that indescribably beautiful touch of his. I also sang 3 of his songs, which seemed to please him... For some time he has been engaged in composing an Opera & an Oratorio, but has lost courage about them. The subject for his Opera is a Rhine Legend, & that for the Oratorio, a very beautiful one depicting Earth, Hell, & Heaven, & he played one of the Choruses out of this to us, which was very fine.*

The opera was clearly *Die Lorelei*, and the oratorio almost certainly *Christus*, the thirteen surviving movements of which were collated after his death by his brother Paul. When the queen asked Mendelssohn if she could fulfil a wish of his in return, the composer asked to be shown the royal children in their nurseries, and Victoria proceeded to give him a personal guided tour. On 4 May Mendelssohn overcame his distaste for Meyerbeer's opera *Robert le diable* to hear Jenny Lind make her London debut in the role of Alice. The occasion was a major event in the city's concert life, and one that would help make proverbial the phrase 'a Jenny Lind crush'. Four days later he left England for the last time, ominously proclaiming: 'One more week of this unremitting fatigue, and I should be killed outright!' Klingemann was worried about him, and insisted on accompanying his friend across the Channel.

Mendelssohn arrived back in Frankfurt on 12 May. Two days later, in Berlin, his sister Fanny was rehearsing *Die erste Walpurgisnacht* for one of her Sunday musicales when she lost feeling in her hands, and recognised the symptoms of a stroke. By the evening she was dead, at the age of forty-one. The news reached her brother in Frankfurt on 18 May. He gave a great cry and collapsed.

There seems no reason to doubt the traditional view that Mendelssohn never recovered from the shock of Fanny's death. Denied even the opportunity of attending her funeral and memorial service, both of which had taken place by the time he learnt of her passing, he descended into a slough of grief. To his brother Paul he confessed:

> It seems to me as if I will only truly be able to believe everything once I have seen and spoken with you. Now I find myself thinking with every footstep I hear, with every letter to be opened, that it might undo what cannot be undone. Or rather I do not think so...

'This will be a changed world for us all now,' he wrote to the shattered Hensel, 'but we must try and get accustomed to the change, though by the time we have got accustomed to it our lives may be over too.'

From the end of May to the middle of September Mendelssohn sought solace with his family, who were joined by Paul's family. They withdrew first to Baden-Baden, where he found the spirit to work on the two Anglican canticles – the *Magnificat* and *Nunc dimittis* for solo voices, choir and organ – that would complete his Three Motets (*Drei Motetten*), Op. 69. (The third piece of the set, *Jubilate Deo*, had already been finished on 5 April.) Next the Mendelssohns settled themselves at Interlaken in Switzerland, where they spent the greater part of the summer. According to the critic Henry Chorley, who visited him there, Felix looked old, sad and stooped. On one occasion he even broke off discussion of *Die Lorelei* with the words, 'But what is the use of planning anything? I shall not live.' He continued work on the opera, however, even while devoting most of his creative energies to watercolours. Then, in the early part of July he began to jot down ideas for a new composition unlike anything he had ever written before.

The String Quartet No. 6 in F minor, Op. 80 was completed in early September, shortly before the Mendelssohn family returned to Leipzig. Dangerous though such biographical readings can be, it is hard not to see in this quartet – the most tormented score Mendelssohn ever wrote – an expression of his anguish at Fanny's death. Gone is the measured Classicism of the Op. 44 quartets. In its place is a language aptly described by Moscheles as an 'agitation of painful feelings', from which only the profoundly elegiac slow movement offers temporary relief. The driven, convulsive lines of the first and last movements hold out scant hope of consolation, and the jagged syncopations of the second movement, *Allegro assai*, are a world away from the characteristic 'Mendelssohnian' scherzo. The quartet is the composer's last major work, and reveals Mendelssohn on the threshold of a new musical world. Two other string quartet movements seemingly date from the same period as the F minor quartet – a Theme and Variations in E major, and a Scherzo in A minor – but they are too isolated to provide much guidance as to what the geography of that world might have been. Unearthed from Mendelssohn's papers after his death, they were cobbled together with the Capriccio in E minor from 1843 and a Fugue in E flat from 1827 to create the spurious semblance of a four-movement quartet, which was published in 1851 as Op. 81.

At the end of September Mendelssohn steeled himself for his first visit to Berlin since Fanny's death. There the sight of her undisturbed room undid all the recuperative effect of his Swiss vacation. Returning to Leipzig, he was unable to face his public and handed over to Gade the opening concerts of the new Gewandhaus season. On 7 October, after completing for publication the Six Songs (*Sechs Lieder*), Op. 71, he wrote a seventh song, 'Altdeutsches Frühlingslied' ('Old German Spring Song'), which would later appear as Op. 86 No. 6. The final verse reads:

> *Nur ich allein, ich leide Pein,*
> *Ohn' Ende werd' ich leiden;*
> *Seit du von mir und ich von dir,*
> *O Liebste, musste scheiden.*

> I alone, I suffer pain,
> I shall suffer without end,
> since I from you and you from me,
> oh my beloved, have to part.

It was his last surviving composition. Two days later, while he was playing through the Op. 71 songs with the soprano Livia Frege, he suffered a stroke. He forced himself to walk home to Königstrasse, where Cécile found him shivering on a sofa, with icy hands and a shattering headache. Over the next few days he seemed to make a good recovery, but on 28 October he suffered a second attack, which confined him to bed. Six days later, on 3 November, a third stroke left him drifting in and out of consciousness. He died at 9.24 on the evening of 4 November.

Crowds had gathered outside the house even before the news of Mendelssohn's death. Now hundreds waited silently in the street to pay their respects. The funeral on 7 November was an occasion of mass public mourning. Moscheles, David, Hauptmann, Gade, Rietz and Schumann accompanied the hearse as, to the strains of the 'Trauermarsch' that Mendelssohn had written for his mother's death in 1842, a procession of thousands of Leipzigers made its way to the Paulinerkirche. There the coffin lay open until the evening, when it was taken by train to Berlin, pausing at Dessau where Moses Mendelssohn had begun his journey to the same city more than a century earlier. The following day another grand cortège accompanied the body to the cemetery of the Trinity Church, where Felix Mendelssohn was buried in the family plot with his sister Fanny by his side.

Personalities

Attwood, Thomas (1765–1838): English composer and organist. A pupil of Mozart's in the 1780s, he was one of Mendelssohn's closest friends in London, arranging access to the organ in St Paul's Cathedral for him and offering hospitality at his house in Norwood.

Beethoven, Ludwig van (1770–1827): German composer. A major influence on Mendelssohn, and one of the very few major composers of his time whom he failed to meet. Beethoven's symphonies formed the core of Mendelssohn's repertoire as a conductor, and Mendelssohn's performances of the Ninth were regarded as revelatory by contemporaries.

Bennett, William Sterndale (1816–1875): English composer and conductor. Mendelssohn rated him very highly and premiered some of his early works at the Gewandhaus concerts. He subsequently became professor of music at Cambridge University and principal of the Royal Academy of Music.

Berlioz, Hector (1803–1869): French composer. Berlioz's admiration for Mendelssohn's music was never reciprocated, but the two men became friends in Rome in 1831 and Mendelssohn organised the Leipzig premiere of Berlioz's *Symphonie fantastique* in 1843. In his colourful *Memoirs* Berlioz famously observed that Mendelssohn was musically 'a little too fond of the dead'.

Casper, Johann Ludwig (1796–1864): Pathologist and Mendelssohn family friend who provided the librettos for Mendelssohn's first four youthful operas, leading Lea Mendelssohn to dub him their 'house poet'.

Cherubini, Luigi (1760–1842): Italian composer, especially of opera and sacred music. Highly regarded in his day by composers as various as Beethoven and Berlioz, as director of the Paris Conservatoire his approval of the young Felix's talent was a crucial factor in persuading Abraham Mendelssohn that his son should pursue a career in music.

Chopin, Fryderyk (1810–1849): Polish composer and pianist greatly admired by Mendelssohn, with whom he became friends in Paris in 1832. Mendelssohn, who was among the first people to hear Chopin's Op. 10 Études, was apt to exempt Chopin from the criticisms he levelled at the virtuoso culture of his time.

David, Ferdinand (1810–1873): German violinist and composer. One of Mendelssohn's closest friends, David became his orchestral leader at the Leipzig Gewandhaus in 1836, a post he held until his death. He is the dedicatee of Mendelssohn's Violin Concerto in E minor, Op. 64 and was the soloist at its premiere in 1845.

Devrient, Eduard (1801–1877): German actor and baritone. A lifelong friend of the composer, he was instrumental in Mendelssohn's 1829 revival of Bach's *St Matthew Passion*. His memoir of the composer, *My Recollections of Felix Mendelssohn Bartholdy*, is a valuable if sometimes theatrical source.

Dirichlet, Rebecka (*née* Mendelssohn) (1811–1858): The composer's younger sister and frequent correspondent. In 1832 she married the eminent mathematician and academic Peter Lejeune Dirichlet (1805–1859).

Frederick Augustus II (1797–1854): King of Saxony (1836–1854). A great admirer of Mendelssohn, on whom he conferred the title of Saxon Kapellmeister in 1841. As director of the Leipzig Gewandhaus concerts, Mendelssohn was the most visible musician working in Frederick Augustus's territories, and persuaded the king to hypothecate funds to the founding of the Leipzig Conservatoire.

Frederick William IV (1795–1861): King of Prussia (1840–1861), who employed Mendelssohn as his music director in Berlin from 1841 to 1844 and kept him on a retainer for special services thereafter. Seen as a reformer when he came to the throne, Frederick William's vacillating cultural and political policies made Mendelssohn's life a misery during his period of service to the royal court.

Gade, Niels (1817–1890): Danish composer. A friend and protégé of Mendelssohn, who premiered Gade's First Symphony, Op. 5 in Leipzig in 1843 and was its dedicatee. Gade deputised for Mendelssohn at the Gewandhaus from 1844 and shared the conducting of the orchestra from 1845.

Mendelssohn turned the conducting of the Gewandhaus Orchestra over to him in 1847. His music has enjoyed a modest revival in recent years.

Goethe, Johann Wolfgang von (1749–1832): German poet and statesman. The most significant German cultural figure of his time, he befriended the twelve-year-old Felix in 1821 and pronounced him a second Mozart. Goethe's work inspired several of Mendelssohn's compositions, including the secular cantata *Die erste Walpurgisnacht* and the overture *Calm Sea and Prosperous Voyage*.

Handley, Delphine (*née* von Schauroth) (1814–1887): Bavarian piano virtuoso. Mendelssohn met her as a fellow prodigy in Paris in 1825 and became romantically attached to her in Munich during his grand tour of Europe from 1829 to 1832. Subsequently the wife of an English clergyman, Delphine was the dedicatee of Mendelssohn's Piano Concerto No. 1, Op. 25.

Hensel, Fanny (*née* Mendelssohn) (1805–1847): Mendelssohn's older sister. A gifted composer and pianist in her own right, she was her brother's musical confidante. Some of her songs were included without attribution in Felix's published collections, but only in the final months of her life did she begin to publish under her own name. The two siblings had a relationship of twin-like closeness, and Queen Victoria was not alone in believing that Fanny's death signed Felix's death warrant. He died six months after her.

Hensel, Wilhelm (1794–1861): Prussian court painter. Mendelssohn's brother-in-law from 1829 when he married Fanny, he left several idealised portraits of the Mendelssohn family and social circle. His personal and professional life was shattered by his wife's death in 1847.

Hensel, Sebastian (1830–1898): Mendelssohn's nephew, the only child of Fanny and Wilhelm Hensel. His memoir *The Mendelssohn Family (1729–1847) from Letters and Journals* is an important, though partial, source for the composer's life.

Hiller, Ferdinand (1811–1885): German composer and conductor. He met Mendelssohn as a fellow child prodigy in 1822, and they remained close friends until differences over Hiller's management of the Leipzig Gewandhaus during Felix's absence in Berlin caused a terminal falling-out in the early 1840s.

Horsley, William (1774–1858): English glee composer. In the course of his many visits to London, Mendelssohn became a close friend of the Horsley family, which included William's son Charles (a student of Mendelssohn's in Leipzig) and his daughters Fanny, Sophy and Mary (the wife of Isambard Kingdom Brunel).

Humboldt, Alexander von (1769–1859): German explorer, scientist and polymath. One of the most comprehensive intellects of his time – his magnum opus *Kosmos* attempts no less than a complete account of the physical universe – Humboldt was a friend of the Berlin Mendelssohns, in whose garden he conducted experiments in terrestrial magnetism. Mendelssohn's 'Humboldt' Cantata was commissioned for the international conference of scientists Humboldt convened in Berlin in 1828. Alexander's brother Wilhelm (1767–1835), diplomat, philologist and first rector of the University of Berlin, was also a friend of the Mendelssohn family.

Immermann, Karl Leberecht (1796–1840): German author and playwright. As director of the municipal theatre, he was instrumental in attracting Mendelssohn to Düsseldorf in 1833. Quarrels between the two men led to Mendelssohn's abrupt resignation as musical supervisor of Immermann's theatre the following year. Immermann is best remembered today as the author of the novel *Münchhausen*, the story of the eponymous baron later immortalised in film and pathology.

Joachim, Joseph (1831–1907): Hungarian violinist, composer and conductor. He was one of the great violin virtuosos of his time. Mendelssohn supported him as a child violinist, introducing him in Leipzig and London, but advised Joachim's guardians to withdraw him from the prodigy circuit for two years to give him time to mature. His relations with Brahms yielded many works including the Violin Concerto, Op. 77.

Klingemann, Karl (1798–1862): Diplomat. One of Mendelssohn's closest friends throughout his life, he was also the composer's librettist on *Heimkehr aus der Fremde* and, as attaché to the Hanoverian legation in London, a key figure in Mendelssohn's English visits. In 1829 Klingemann accompanied Mendelssohn on the tour of Scotland that inspired both *The Hebrides* and the 'Scottish' Symphony.

Lind, Jenny (1820–1887): Stockholm-born soprano, known as the 'Swedish Nightingale'. Famed for her purity of voice and seemingly uncalculated simplicity of manner, she made a profound impression on Mendelssohn, who introduced her to the Leipzig Gewandhaus in 1845. He designed the soprano part of *Elijah* for her, though she never sang it under his direction. The closeness of their relationship was the subject of much comment at the time, as it has continued to be since. In 1852 she married the conductor Otto Goldschmidt, who had been a student of Mendelssohn's at the Leipzig Conservatoire.

Liszt, Franz (1811–1886): Hungarian composer and virtuoso pianist. Mendelssohn first met him in Paris in 1825 and dismissed him as having 'many fingers, but little brains'. Though he later came to admire his technical skill, Mendelssohn remained suspicious of Liszt's showmanship, which he recognised as a new phenomenon (and which upstaged several of his own appearances in Berlin in 1841). Most of the compositions for which Liszt is now known were written after Mendelssohn's death.

Marx, Adolf Bernhard (1795–1866): German music critic and theorist. One of the most significant influences on the young Mendelssohn, Marx claimed credit for advising him on the composition of *A Midsummer Night's Dream* overture. Marx's views on the descriptive power of music were influential in shaping the broadly programmatic nature of some of Mendelssohn's best-known works, including the overtures *Calm Sea and Prosperous Voyage* and *The Hebrides*. The two fell out in 1840, from which point Marx became a bitter critic of his former friend.

Mendelssohn, Abraham (1776–1835): Felix's father; co-founder with his brother Joseph (1770–1848) of Mendelssohn Brothers Bank, which remained a major force in the German financial markets until its forced closure by the Nazis in 1938. In many respects an unfulfilled figure – 'Formerly I was known as the son of my father; now I am known as the father of my son,' he once wrote – he was the most powerful influence on Felix's upbringing, education and career decisions as a professional musician.

Mendelssohn, Cécile (*née* Jeanrenaud) (1817–1853): The composer's wife (from 1837) and mother of his five children. As the daughter of a prominent Huguenot family in Frankfurt, her background was similar to her husband's in being at once patrician and semi-detached from the dominant religious culture. Cécile emerges from the shadows principally through the pages of the Mendelssohns' joint honeymoon diary.

Mendelssohn, Lea (*née* Salomon) (1777–1842): Felix's mother. As the granddaughter of Daniel Itzig, financier to Frederick the Great and the first Jew to be granted Prussian citizenship, she brought to her marriage a set of family connections grander even than her husband's. She was an accomplished musician and gave Felix and Fanny their first piano lessons.

Mendelssohn, Moses (1729–1786): Felix's grandfather, born Moses ben Mendel Dessau. Philosopher, author and unofficial ambassador for European Jewry, he was a key figure of the Enlightenment and the model for the eponymous hero of Lessing's play *Nathan the Wise*. In addition to his other accomplishments, he seems to have taken music lessons from J.P. Kirnberger, a pupil of J.S. Bach.

Mendelssohn, Paul (1812–1874): Felix's brother. An able cellist, for whom Mendelssohn wrote, among other works, his Cello Sonata No. 2, Op. 58, he followed his father into the banking business and handled Felix's financial affairs.

Moscheles, Ignaz (1794–1870): Bohemian-born composer, pianist and conductor. Astonished by Felix's talents as a boy, he became a close friend of the mature composer and often appeared on the concert platform with him in London and elsewhere. In 1833 he co-wrote with Mendelssohn the *Variations brillantes* on the gypsy march from Weber's incidental music to P.A. Wolff's *Preciosa*. At Mendelssohn's invitation he became professor of piano at the Leipzig Conservatoire from 1846. Moscheles's son Felix was Mendelssohn's godson.

Rietz, Eduard (1802–1832): German violinist. Entering the Mendelssohn household as Felix's violin teacher around 1820, he quickly became a friend and was the dedicatee of Mendelssohn's first masterpiece, the Octet, Op. 20. His early death prompted Mendelssohn to write the Intermezzo of the String Quintet, Op. 18 in his memory. Rietz's cellist brother Julius (1812–1877) was an able deputy to Mendelssohn as conductor of the theatre orchestra in Düsseldorf, which he took over on Felix's resignation in 1834.

Rosen, Friedrich (1805–1837): German orientalist. A member of the Mendelssohn circle in Berlin, he later settled in London, where he pursued an academic career. He was one of the composer's closest friends in the city and a regular correspondent. Rosen's younger sister Sophie, who married Felix's friend Karl Klingemann, is the dedicatee of the last collection of *Songs without Words* to be published during Mendelssohn's lifetime (Op. 67).

Schadow, Wilhelm von (1788–1862): German painter. He was associated in Rome with the Nazarene circle of artists around Felix's maternal uncle Jacob Bartholdy. As director of the

Düsseldorf Academy of Arts he was a supportive friend and sometime landlord to Mendelssohn during his difficult music directorship in the Rhineland town. Schadow's 1834 pencil drawing is perhaps the most speaking likeness of a composer who died just too early to be routinely photographed.

Schelble, Johann Nepomuk (1789–1837): German conductor. He was an early advocate of Bach's neglected choral music, and as director of the Frankfurt Cäcilienverein he commissioned Mendelssohn's first oratorio, *St Paul*. The composer stood in for him at the Cäcilienverein during Schelble's final illness.

Schlegel, Dorothea (*née* Brendel Mendelssohn) (1764–1839): The most colourful of Felix's formidable battery of aunts, Dorothea was the one whom he saw most in adulthood. A scandalous figure following her divorce and high-profile affair with the writer Friedrich Schlegel, she was nonetheless the only member of the Mendelssohn family present at her nephew's wedding in 1837.

Schubring, Julius (1806–1889): German theologian. A friend from childhood days, Schubring collaborated with Mendelssohn on the librettos of his two oratorios, *St Paul* and *Elijah*.

Schumann, Clara (*née* Wieck) (1819–1896): German pianist and composer. A child prodigy when Mendelssohn met her in Paris in 1825, she became a close friend and musical colleague during his time at the Leipzig Gewandhaus. A keen interpreter of Mendelssohn's music, she was the dedicatee of the most famous of his *Songs without Words*, the 'Spring Song', Op. 62 No. 6, which she did much to popularise. Mendelssohn wrote the *Allegro brillant* for piano duet, Op.

92, for her debut performance with her husband Robert, whom she married in 1840.

Schumann, Robert (1810–1856): German composer. A friend and associate of Mendelssohn from the latter's arrival in Leipzig in 1835, he ardently advocated Mendelssohn's music in the pages of his journal *Die Neue Zeitschrift für Musik*. Mendelssohn premiered Schumann's Symphonies Nos 1 and 2 at the Gewandhaus, as well as Schubert's 'Great' C major Symphony, which Schumann had unearthed and brought to his attention. Schumann's increasing mental instability taxed relations between the two men towards the end of Mendelssohn's life.

Spohr, Louis (1784 –1859): German composer and violinist. Much admired by Mendelssohn, who performed several of his works at the Gewandhaus, Spohr was the dedicatee of the Piano Trio No. 2, Op. 66. He dedicated his own Piano Sonata, Op. 125 to Mendelssohn.

Spontini, Gaspare (1774–1851): Italian opera composer. As musical director of the Berlin Schauspielhaus he obstructed Felix's early career in the city despite his close links with Mendelssohn's *salonnière* aunts. His delay in mounting Mendelssohn's only opera to reach the public stage, *Die Hochzeit des Camacho*, may have contributed to its failure. A notoriously prickly figure, he was dismissed for *lèse majesté* under Frederick William IV.

Tieck, Ludwig (1773–1853): German dramatist and translator. His translations, with August Wilhelm Schlegel, of Shakespeare's plays were a landmark in German cultural life. Like Mendelssohn, Tieck was poached from Saxony by

Frederick William IV of Prussia, whose 'chief court reader' he became. Mendelssohn's collaboration with him in a series of court productions in Berlin produced the incidental music to *Antigone, Athalie, Oedipus at Colonos* and *A Midsummer Night's Dream*.

Wagner, Richard (1813–1883): German composer. Avowedly an early admirer of Mendelssohn, whom he met on several occasions, in 1850 he was the pseudonymous author of the article *Über das Judentum in der Musik* ('On Judaism in Music'), which notoriously embedded anti-Semitism in the Mendelssohn critical tradition. Mendelssohn had little time for Wagner's music, and the only occasion on which he conducted any (the Overture to *Tannhäuser* in 1846) was apparently a disaster.

Weber, Carl Maria von (1786–1826): German composer, and friend of the Mendelssohn family. The Berlin premiere of Weber's *Der Freischütz* in 1821 was a landmark event in Felix's life, and Weber remained a significant influence on the younger composer's music. Weber's *Konzertstück* was a staple of Mendelssohn's repertoire as a pianist.

Zelter, Carl Friedrich (1758–1832): German conductor, composer and teacher. As Felix's principal music tutor from 1819, he was the single most significant formative influence on the young composer, whom he introduced to his friend Goethe in 1821. Zelter was director of Berlin's Singakademie from 1800 until his death, after which Mendelssohn stood for election to the post but was defeated. Anti-Semitic comments in Zelter's posthumously published correspondence with Goethe clouded the Mendelssohns' memories of him.

Selected Bibliography

Blunt, Wilfred, *On Wings of Song: A Biography of Felix Mendelssohn*, New York, 1974

Citron, Marcia J., ed. & trans., *The Letters of Fanny Hensel to Felix Mendelssohn*, Stuyvesant, 1987

Devrient, Eduard, trans. Natalia Macfarren, *My Recollections of Felix Mendelssohn Bartholdy and his Letters to Me*, London, 1869, repr. New York, 1972

Elvers, Rudolf, ed., trans. Craig Tomlinson, *Felix Mendelssohn: A Life in Letters*, London, 1986

Hiller, Ferdinand, trans. M.E. von Glehn, *Felix Mendelssohn Bartholdy: Letters and Recollections*, London, 1874, repr. New York, 1972

Köhler, Karl-Heinz, 'Felix Mendelssohn' in *The New Grove Early Romantic Masters*, London, 1985

Kupferberg, Herbert, *The Mendelssohns: Three Generations of Genius*, London & New York, 1972

Marek, George R., *Gentle Genius: The Story of Felix Mendelssohn*, London & New York, 1972

Mercer-Taylor, Peter, ed., *The Cambridge Companion to Mendelssohn*, Cambridge, 2004

Mercer-Taylor, Peter, *The Life of Mendelssohn*, Cambridge, 2000

Moshansky, Mozelle, *Mendelssohn* ('Illustrated Lives of the Great Composers'), London, 1982

Nichols, Roger, ed., *Mendelssohn Remembered*, London, 1997

Radcliffe, Philip, *Mendelssohn* ('The Master Musicians Series'), London, 1954, 3rd ed. rev. Peter Ward Jones, London, 1990

Selden-Goth, G., ed., *Felix Mendelssohn: Letters*, New York, 1945, repr. 1972

Todd, R. Larry, *Mendelssohn: A Life in Music*, Oxford & New York, 2003

Todd, R. Larry, Mendelssohn entry in Stanley Sadie & John Tyrrell, eds, *The New Grove Dictionary of Music and Musicians*, London, 2nd ed. 2001

Todd, R. Larry, *Mendelssohn: The Hebrides and other Overtures*, Cambridge, 1993

Todd, R. Larry, ed., *Mendelssohn and his World*, Princeton, 1991

Ward Jones, Peter, ed. & trans., *The Mendelssohns on Honeymoon: The 1837 Diary of Felix and Cécile Mendelssohn Bartholdy Together with Letters to their Families*, Oxford, 1997

Werner, Eric, trans. Dika Newlin, *Mendelssohn: A New Image of the Composer and his Age*, London & New York, 1963

Glossary

Absolute music Music without an underlying programme or extra-musical meaning, as against 'programme music' (see below).

A cappella For unaccompanied voices.

Antiphony The deployment of two parts of a choir alternately, each answering the other. Music of this kind is described as antiphonal.

Appassionato Impassioned.

Arpeggio A chord spread so that the notes are played one after another, usually from the bottom up. A chord so played is said to be arpeggiated.

Autograph A composer's original manuscript score.

Barcarolle Boatman's song, effectively interchangeable with the term 'Gondellied' (see below) in Mendelssohn's music.

Cadenza A virtuoso display by the soloist in a concerto, sometimes improvised and typically occurring between the end of the recapitulation and the coda. In Mendelssohn's Violin Concerto, Op. 64 the cadenza famously introduces the recapitulation.

Canon An imitative musical device in which a single theme is played or sung by two or more voices starting one after another, as in the well-known round *Frère Jacques*.

Cantata A sacred or secular work in several movements for accompanied voice or voices. Mendelssohn's cantatas include *Die erste Walpurgisnacht* and several Psalm settings. He designated the hybrid *Lobgesang* ('Hymn of Praise') a 'symphony-cantata'.

Cantor Director of music in Protestant churches, often also having a teaching role. It was one of Mendelssohn's terms of affection and respect for his older sister Fanny.

Cavatina An instrumental piece with the characteristics of a simple song.

Chorale Type of hymn tune associated especially with the Lutheran Church in Germany and designed to be sung by the whole congregation; J.S. Bach's cantatas employ several chorales. Mendelssohn used chorales or chorale-like melodies in works such as *St Paul* and the 'Reformation' and *Lobgesang* symphonies.

Coda The tailpiece at the end of a sonata-form movement, following the recapitulation.

Concert overture Overture intended to stand alone rather than as the curtain-raiser to an opera or other dramatic work. Mendelssohn's contributions to the form, including *The Hebrides* and *Calm Sea and Prosperous Voyage*, were highly influential in establishing its popularity in the nineteenth century.

Continuo A shortening of 'basso continuo' – continuous bass. The use of a keyboard to underpin the harmony of an instrumental or choral work, associated especially with Baroque music.

Counterpoint The interweaving of two or more separate horizontal lines of melody played together. Music in which counterpoint occurs is described as contrapuntal.

Development The middle section of a sonata-form movement (coming between the exposition and the recapitulation) in which the thematic material of the exposition is developed.

Exposition The first main section of a sonata-form movement in which the thematic material, typically including two or more subjects, is set out and sometimes repeated.

Fugato Music having some of the characteristics of fugue (see below).

Fugue A rigorous form of counterpoint in which several musical 'voices' imitate one another, each entering in succession after the first voice has stated the subject or theme. When the second voice presents the subject, the first continues with a new subsidiary theme known as the countersubject.

Glee A type of simply harmonised part-song for three or more male voices, popular in England in the early nineteenth century. Mendelssohn's friend William Horsley was a leading exponent of the form.

Gondellied Gondolier's song, a type of Barcarolle, which term is often used interchangeably with it. Mendelssohn's *Songs without Words* include several characteristic examples.

Intermezzo A movement or section that functions as an interlude. Originally a comic episode between main sections of an opera, it soon came to be used in instrumental works.

Kapelle   By extension from the German for chapel, the collective name for the musicians associated with a royal chapel or court.

Kapellmeister   The director of a Kapelle (see above), thus effectively 'music director'. Mendelssohn was at different times, and temporarily at the same time, Kapellmeister to the courts of Saxony and Prussia.

Leggierissimo   Very lightly.

Lento   Slowly.

Libretto   Literally 'little book'. The words of an opera or oratorio.

Liederspiel   A quasi-operatic entertainment consisting of a series of linked songs. Mendelssohn's *Heimkehr aus der Fremde* is an example of the form.

Maestoso   Majestic.

Modulation   Moving from one key to another.

Oratorio   A large-scale unstaged sacred or secular dramatic work for solo singers, choir and orchestra. Mendelssohn's *St Paul* and *Elijah* were the pre-eminent nineteenth-century examples of the form.

Pentatonic   A five-note scale, such as that produced by playing the black notes on the piano. Melodic material based on the pentatonic scale is typical of much folk music, and features in the scherzo of Mendelssohn's 'Scottish' Symphony.

Programme music Illustrative music with a specific or implied narrative underlying it, in contrast to 'absolute music' (see above). Mendelssohn's overtures *A Midsummer Night's Dream*, *Calm Sea and Prosperous Voyage* and *The Hebrides* are early Romantic examples.

Recapitulation The section in a sonata-form movement in which the material of the exposition is reprised in amended form. It follows the development section and is sometimes itself followed by a coda.

Recitative Passage of free declamation in opera or other vocal work, and by extension an instrumental passage having the same characteristics.

Rondo A musical form, often used in the last movement of a work, in which a theme stated at the beginning makes repeated appearances, separated by contrasting episodes.

Saltarello Italian leaping dance. The finale of Mendelssohn's 'Italian' Symphony is built on its characteristic rhythms.

Scherzando Playfully.

Scherzo Literally 'joke', typically the liveliest (third or second) movement of a symphony, string quartet, piano sonata, etc. Mendelssohn's scherzos often tap the 'elfin' vein associated with the overture *A Midsummer Night's Dream*.

Siciliano Literally 'Sicilian', a kind of lilting pastoral song often imported into instrumental art-music from the Baroque period onwards.

Singspiel Operatic work, usually comic in subject, consisting of spoken dialogue and sung numbers. Mendelssohn composed four such works in his early youth.

Sonata form The most characteristic form for an opening movement, and often other movements too, in a Classical sonata, symphony, etc. In its most regular form it consists of three sections: the exposition (in which the thematic material is set out), the development (in which its potential is explored and developed) and the recapitulation (in which the material of the exposition is reprised in amended form).

Syncopation A pattern of emphasis imposed against the natural rhythm of the music, for example by the accenting of weak beats.

Ternary Having three connected sections, the third being (more or less) a repeat of the first. Also known as A–B–A form.

Transposition The exact reproduction of a passage or work in a key different from that of the original.

Trio Both a work for three instruments and the contrasting middle section of a scherzo or minuet movement.

Trio sonata Baroque chamber music form, typically composed for two melody instruments (e.g. violin, oboe or flute) and a bass instrument (e.g. cello or bassoon) with keyboard continuo (see 'continuo' above).

Vaudeville French sub-operatic theatrical entertainment, typically featuring spoken dialogue and popular songs. Mendelssohn's early Singspiels are influenced by the form. During the later part of the nineteenth century vaudeville mutated into music hall and variety shows.

Annotations of CD Tracks

CD 1

☐1☐ String Symphony No. 8 in D major. **Movement 4: Allegro molto**

The thirteen symphonies for strings that Mendelssohn wrote between September 1821 and December 1823 stand at the heart of his output as a child composer. The String Symphony No. 8 was completed on 27 November 1822, when he was just thirteen years old. In many ways the most remarkable of all the string symphonies – or sinfonias, as he designated them – it is also perhaps the most astonishing work ever to proceed from the pen of so young a composer (Mozart and Rossini not excepted). The finale, in particular, is a dizzying *tour de force* of contrapuntal writing, directly inspired by one of the towering achievements of western music, the finale of Mozart's 'Jupiter' Symphony, K. 551, which held a lifelong fascination for Mendelssohn. Felix arranged the String Symphony for full orchestra shortly after completing it, creating in the process his earliest orchestral symphony, but the recording heard here is the original version for strings.

☐2☐ Octet in E flat major, Op. 20. **Movement 1: Allegro moderato, ma con fuoco**

The Octet is Mendelssohn's first masterpiece and one of the finest chamber works of the nineteenth century. Dated 15 October 1825, it was written when he was sixteen years old, shortly after the family's move to their palatial new property at 3 Leipzigerstrasse in Berlin. Sir George Grove described its composition as Mendelssohn's 'wonderful leap into maturity', and the Octet stands witness to his status as probably the greatest child genius in the history of music. Even the medium of the string octet as Mendelssohn deploys it here is unprecedented. Spohr had written double quartets, but Mendelssohn treats each of his instruments as an individual voice from the very first bars, in which the upsurging main theme, announced by the first violin, spans a compass of almost three octaves. The closing bars of the first movement exposition, in which the first violin soars rapturously above the other instruments as they recall the arpeggios of the main theme, are among the most exhilarating in all chamber music. The Octet was dedicated to Mendelssohn's friend and one-time violin teacher Eduard Rietz.

3 A Midsummer Night's Dream (overture), Op. 21

The overture *A Midsummer Night's Dream* was written less than a year after the Octet, in the summer of 1826, a particularly happy period in Felix's life. The seventeen-year-old composer had read Shakespeare's play in the German translation by August Wilhelm Schlegel, and the overture (the second masterpiece of Mendelssohn's youth) captures perfectly the enchanted world of the 'wood near Athens'. It opens with four magical wind chords, which punctuate the sonata form, returning at the start of the recapitulation and again at the very end of the work. The contrasting themes of the exposition represent the fairies, Theseus' courtiers, the lovers, and the antics of the 'hempen homespuns', including Bottom, whose transmogrified brays can be heard from the ophicleide – one of several touches the music critic A.B. Marx claimed to have suggested to the composer. In 1843 Mendelssohn redeployed the overture in his incidental music for *A Midsummer Night's Dream*, Op. 61, adding thirteen new numbers (including the 'Notturno': see CD 2, track 7), several of which also derive their thematic material from the overture.

4 String Quartet No. 2 in A minor, Op. 13. **Movement 1: Adagio – Allegro vivace**

Composed in Berlin in the autumn of 1827, Mendelssohn's String Quartet in A minor is the earliest of the five string quartets published during his lifetime and its questing idiom stands without precedent or sequel in his output. On 17 February 1835 Mendelssohn's sister Fanny wrote to him, 'we were young precisely in the time of Beethoven's last years, and it was only to be expected that we completely assimilated his manner, as it is so moving and impressive. But you have lived through it and written yourself through it.' The A minor quartet represents the young Mendelssohn's most intense engagement with Beethoven's late style, as epitomised in the Viennese master's final string quartets. The first movement begins with a searching *Adagio* introduction based on the motif that accompanies the words 'Ist es wahr?' ('Is it true?') in Mendelssohn's song *Frage* ('Question'), written in the summer of 1827. Probably associated with Mendelssohn's feelings for Betty Pistor, the young singer to whom he dedicated his next string quartet, the motif recurs in the *Adagio non lento* that closes the finale of the work, thus framing the whole quartet.

5   Three Fantasies or Caprices, Op. 16. **No. 2 in E minor: Scherzo: Presto**

Written for the daughters of his friend the mine owner John Taylor, with whom he stayed in north Wales during his first visit to the British Isles in 1829, the charming keyboard miniatures that make up the Three Fantasies or Caprices (*Trois fantaisies ou caprices*) were among Mendelssohn's own favourite piano compositions. The second piece, a fleeting scherzo in his characteristic 'elfin' vein, was written for Honora Taylor and was intended to represent a plant in her garden with trumpet-shaped flowers, hence the fanfare-like opening. It found an unlikely later incarnation as the music that accompanies Toto's escape from the Wicked Witch of the West in the classic 1939 film *The Wizard of Oz*.

6   Songs without Words, Op. 19b.
    No. 6 in G minor, 'Venetianisches Gondellied' ('Venetian Gondolier's Song')

Mendelssohn published six collections of *Songs without Words*, each containing six piano pieces, and two more collections appeared after his death. This hypnotic miniature, one of the earliest of the 'songs', dates from October 1830 and was composed in Venice, the first stop on the Italian leg of his grand tour of Europe. Mendelssohn's first 'Gondellied' or 'gondolier's song', it was written for the young pianist Delphine von Schauroth, whom he had met and become infatuated with in Munich earlier on the tour, and to whom he would later dedicate his Piano Concerto No. 1, also in G minor. The lapping rhythms are a gently melancholy evocation of the Venetian canals, and perhaps also reflect the composer's mood at his separation from Delphine. The 'Gondellied' was included as the final piece in Mendelssohn's first collection of *Songs without Words*, which was published in 1832.

7 The Hebrides (Fingal's Cave), Op. 26

The Hebrides also dates from Mendelssohn's cultural grand tour of Europe. Sometimes also known as *Fingal's Cave*, it was begun in 1829 on a walking holiday in Scotland with his friend Karl Klingemann before they had actually visited the eponymous cave. It underwent a long and complex evolution (and several changes of title) before reaching the form in which it was published, together with the *Midsummer Night's Dream* and *Calm Sea and Prosperous Voyage* overtures, in 1835. The overture begins in the simplest and most evocative manner, with a threefold statement of the mysterious main theme at progressively higher pitches. A swelling second subject is introduced in the cellos and taken up by the violins, and in the development section, which is heralded by brass fanfares, a new and slightly sinister figure asserts itself in the winds. The recapitulation develops the thematic material further, and there is a stormy coda before the music subsides, dying away in distant echoes of the opening motif.

8 Symphony No. 4 in A major, Op. 90 'Italian'. Movement 1: Allegro vivace

Like *The Hebrides*, Mendelssohn's 'Italian' Symphony has its origins in the tour of Europe he undertook between 1829 and 1832, though it was completed only in 1833 in response to a commission from the Philharmonic Society of London, where he conducted the premiere on 13 May that year. Never satisfied with the work, Mendelssohn left it unpublished at his death, since when it has established itself as one of the best-loved symphonies in the repertoire. The first movement is one of his most effervescent creations, the violins singing the opening theme over a pulsing accompaniment in the winds with an ebullience inescapably redolent of what Felix described to his sister Fanny as 'the land of bright skies and warmth'. In the development a light-footed fugato builds to a stamping climax, after which the music sinks into sudden sadness before the main theme bursts through the clouds once more at the beginning of the recapitulation. In order of composition the third of Mendelssohn's five mature symphonies, the 'Italian' was published as No. 4 in 1851.

9 – 10 Six Preludes and Fugues, Op. 35
    Prelude No. 1 in E minor
    Fugue No. 1 in E minor

The Six Preludes and Fugues for piano, Op. 35 were published in 1837, the year of Mendelssohn's marriage to Cécile Jeanrenaud and a time of great happiness and professional success for the composer. Modelled on Bach's *Well-tempered Clavier*, Op. 35 is one of Mendelssohn's most substantial contributions to the literature of the piano, and brings together material written over several years. The earliest of all is this Fugue No. 1, in E minor, which the composer conceived at the bedside of a dying friend, August Hanstein, in June 1827. Its angular lines and accelerating counterpoint convey something of his anguish at the relentless progress of the invalid's disease. At its climax, the fugue breaks out unexpectedly into an original chorale theme, in E major, as if by way of benediction on the departed. The Prelude, composed in 1835 and marked *Allegro con fuoco*, is an example of the 'three-hand' technique, a speciality of Mendelssohn's contemporary the virtuoso Sigismond Thalberg. In it, the theme is played by the thumbs in the centre of a web of arpeggiated harmony. The American pianist and critic Charles Rosen has described Op. 35 No. 1 as one of the unequivocal masterpieces amongst Mendelssohn's keyboard works.

CD 2

1 String Quartet No. 5 in E flat major, Op. 44 No. 3
Movement 2: Scherzo: Assai leggiero vivace

The three quartets published together as Mendelssohn's Op. 44 all date from the first year or so of his married life and have often been seen as representing a re-engagement with Classical forms and procedures. The second in order of composition, the E flat major quartet was conceived in the weeks following his and Cécile's return from their honeymoon in May 1837. By 22 July Felix could write to his sister Fanny that the new work was almost complete in his head, though it was not finally committed to paper until the following year (the score is dated 6 February 1838, the day before the birth of Mendelssohn's first child). The inner movements of the quartet are particularly fine. The second, this highly original Scherzo, is cast in rondo form. Here, the elves of so many previous scherzos seem metamorphosed into whirling dust devils.

2 Piano Trio No. 1 in D minor, Op. 49. **Movement 2: Andante con moto tranquillo**

It was in reviewing the Piano Trio No. 1 that Robert Schumann famously pronounced Mendelssohn 'the Mozart of the nineteenth century, the most brilliant musician, the one who most clearly sees through the contradictions of the age and for the first time reconciles them'. Written in the summer of 1839, the trio is cut from the same Classicising cloth as the Op. 44 quartets and has always been among Mendelssohn's most popular chamber works. The ternary slow movement, in B flat major, is one of his most characteristic inspirations. The lyrical main theme, announced by the piano and taken up by the other instruments, could easily belong to one of his *Songs without Words*. The piano also introduces the more agitated central section, after which the opening theme returns on the violin, ushering in a recapitulation of the first section and bringing the movement to a radiantly peaceful conclusion.

[3] Variations sérieuses in D minor, Op. 54

The *Variations sérieuses* – Mendelssohn's masterpiece for piano – was composed in 1841 as his contribution to an album of piano pieces intended to raise funds for a Beethoven monument in Bonn. As the title suggests, the variations eschew mere showmanship in favour of a profoundly serious exploration of the possibilities of their theme, which is a plaintive chromatic melody of Mendelssohn's own composition. The eighteen variations bring to bear the full weight of Mendelssohn's compositional experience. No. 4 is a two-part canon, No. 10 a fugato on a single motif from the theme. There are shades of Schumann in the misty sonorities of No. 11, while No. 13 deploys the 'three-hand' technique Mendelssohn had used to such effect in the Prelude, Op. 35 No. 1 (see CD 1, track 9). The following variation, the hymn-like No. 14, arrests the forward momentum of the work in an episode of timeless repose at the emotional heart of the work. The pace gathers again in Nos 15 and 16 and reaches a dramatic climax in No. 17, where the theme is restated over an ominous tremolo in the bass. The final variation is a sort of virtuosic coda, after which the work ends on a note of weariness, all passion spent.

[4] Symphony No. 3 in A minor, Op. 56 'Scottish'
Movement 4: Allegro vivacissimo – Allegro maestoso assai

The last of Mendelssohn's five mature symphonies, the 'Scottish' was the third to be published in his lifetime. It had one of the longest gestations of any of his works. On 30 July 1829, at the beginning of his Scottish walking tour with Klingemann, Mendelssohn visited the ruined chapel at Holyrood where Mary Queen of Scots was crowned. 'I believe,' he wrote home to his family, 'I found today in that old chapel the beginning of my Scottish Symphony.' It would be almost thirteen years before he completed it, however, dating the score in Berlin on 20 January 1842. The last movement of the symphony is perhaps Mendelssohn's most successful symphonic finale. After a sonata form marked by extensive contrapuntal development, the music dies away and a coda unexpectedly introduces a completely new theme of distinctly Scottish cut – though in fact derived from the opening phrase of the soprano solo at the beginning of the *Ave Maria* of 1830, Op. 23 No. 2 – which builds to a rousing climax, as of a celebratory gathering of the clans.

5 Children's Pieces (Christmas Pieces), Op. 72
No. 2: Andante sostenuto

'Do you also have such nice sledge runs as we have here?' Mendelssohn wrote to his six-year-old nephew Sebastian Hensel in February 1829. 'If so you must have been quite thrilled. I find it lovely that you have seen an elephant; they are my favourite animals, so strong and powerful and yet so gentle and friendly and wise. Someday you too must become so.' The letter is testimony to his much-remarked affinity with children, which found expression three years later in the six *Children's Pieces* (*Kinderstücke*, also known as the 'Christmas Pieces'). These delightful piano miniatures were written for the children of his wife's relatives the Beneckes, with whom Felix and Cécile were staying near London during their first joint visit to England in the summer of 1842. The pieces, which breathe the same atmosphere as Schumann's *Kinderszenen* of 1838, have a freshness denied by over-familiarity to the contemporary 'Spring Song', Op. 62 No. 6.

6 Songs without Words, Op. 62
No. 3 in E minor: 'Trauermarsch' ('Funeral March')

The fifth of the six collections of *Songs without Words* published during Mendelssohn's lifetime, Op. 62 contains a piece which perhaps carries the most emotional weight of any of his essays in the genre. Composed on 19 January 1843, the 'Funeral March', as it has come to be known, reflects Mendelssohn's grief at the sudden death of his mother Lea the previous month. The opening fanfares, strikingly prophetic of the funeral march in Mahler's Fifth Symphony, introduce a solemn processional that – in a version for wind band by Mendelssohn's friend and colleague Ignaz Moscheles – would accompany the composer's coffin on his own final journey five years later.

7. A Midsummer Night's Dream (incidental music), Op. 61. **No. 7: Notturno**

Mendelssohn's return to Shakespeare's *A Midsummer Night's Dream* in 1843, seventeen years after he wrote his youthful overture (see CD 1, track 3), was the result of a commission from King Frederick William IV of Prussia during Mendelssohn's unhappy period of service as Kapellmeister in Berlin. Asked to provide incidental music for a new staging of the play in collaboration with the poet and Shakespeare translator Ludwig Tieck, Mendelssohn added thirteen numbers to the overture, including four entr'actes. These are often performed as separate concert items (the last of them being the ubiquitous 'Wedding March'). The exquisite 'Notturno' was intended as the entr'acte between Acts 3 and 4 and evokes the sleeping lovers in the heart of the enchanted forest. It is composed in ternary form, the outer sections, with their magical writing for the horn, framing a more restless central section in which we seem to eavesdrop on the lovers' uneasy dreams.

8. Violin Concerto in E minor, Op. 64. **Movement 1: Allegro molto appassionato**

On 30 July 1838 Mendelssohn wrote to his old friend Ferdinand David (who was the leader of his Leipzig orchestra): 'I'd like to do a violin concerto for you for next winter; one in E minor is running through my head, and the opening will not leave me in peace.' The work was not completed, however, until the summer of 1844, which Mendelssohn spent with his family in Soden, near Frankfurt. That opening idea, first announced by the soloist over murmuring strings and then taken up by the full orchestra, has haunted millions as it haunted the composer. Perhaps the most striking formal feature of the first movement of the Violin Concerto, however, is Mendelssohn's handling of the cadenza. Conventionally in a mid-nineteenth-century concerto, the cadenza would occur at the end of the recapitulation and would be improvised by the soloist. Mendelssohn, however, places it at the end of the development section and writes it out fully. What follows is one of the most magical moments in all music as, towards the end of the cadenza, from behind the violin's rapid hushed arpeggios, the main theme emerges quietly in the orchestra at the beginning of the recapitulation.

9. Organ Sonata, Op. 65 No. 3 in A major. **Movement 1: Con moto maestoso**

As one of the greatest organists of his time Mendelssohn was especially celebrated for his improvisations, which drew crowds to St Paul's Cathedral when he played the organ there during his visits to London. A cornerstone of the organ repertoire, the six Organ Sonatas, Op. 65 have their origins in an 1844 commission from the English publisher Coventry & Hollier for a series of 'voluntaries'. The sonatas were completed on 2 April 1845 and published later the same year under the strapline 'Mendelssohn's School of Organ Playing'. The Third Sonata is unusual in having only two movements (the rest have either three or four). The first movement begins with a processional probably originally intended for his sister Fanny's wedding to Wilhelm Hensel sixteen years earlier. The ensuing fugue is based on the recitative 'Watchman, will the night soon pass?' (No. 6) from his own *Lobgesang* Symphony of 1840, and features in the pedal part the chorale 'Aus tiefer Noth schrei ich zu dir' ('Out of the depths have I cried unto thee'), which Mendelssohn had set in October 1830 as the first of his *Drei Kirchenmusik* – Op. 23. The movement ends, as it began, with the celebratory processional.

10. Elijah, Op. 70. **Aria: 'It is enough' (Elijah)**

Mendelssohn had first discussed the possibility of an oratorio on the subject of the Old Testament prophet Elijah at least as early as 1837, when he and his friend Karl Klingemann began to collaborate on a libretto during Mendelssohn's visit to London in the months after his marriage. Subsequent discussions with Julius Schubring, who had assisted him with the libretto of his previous oratorio *St Paul*, were abandoned in 1839 when the composer found himself too busy to pursue the project. However, they were revived in 1845 in response to a commission from the Birmingham Musical Festival, where *Elijah* received its triumphant premiere on 26 August 1846. The English version of the libretto was prepared by William Bartholomew, who was also responsible for the paraphrase of Psalm 55 *Hear My Prayer*, which Mendelssohn famously set in January 1844. The major work of Mendelssohn's last years, *Elijah* has sometimes been seen as a kind of surrogate for the mature opera he was never to write. The prophet's despairing aria 'It is enough'

(No. 26) after his flight into the wilderness in Part 2 has sometimes been taken as a reflection of Mendelssohn's own world-weariness at the time of its composition.

⑪ String Quartet No. 6 in F minor, Op. 80. **Movement 1: Allegro assai – Presto**

The String Quartet in F minor, from early September 1847, is Mendelssohn's last major composition. Completed just two months before his untimely death, it shows the composer standing on the threshold of a new musical world. Its convulsive, dissonant language is unprecedented in his work and many critics have seen in it a reflection of his anguish at the death of his beloved sister Fanny in May of the same year. The first movement, with its relentless driving rhythms and dislocated motivic material, is typical of what Moscheles referred to as the quartet's 'agitation of painful feelings' – an idiom that seems at times to anticipate the future sound-world of Smetana's quartets. The quartet was not published until after the composer's death, but Mendelssohn's corrections to the score suggest that he fully intended to issue it in print had he lived.

Index

Also Available

Mozart

Beethoven

Chopin

Mahler

Tchaikovsky

Wagner

Puccini

Dvořák